**SOUTH CAMPUS LIBRARY
TARRANT COUNTY
JUNIOR COLLEGE
FT. WORTH, TEXAS 76119**

JOHN GREENLEAF WHITTIER

JOHN GREENLEAF WHITTIER

HIS LIFE AND WORK

BY

GEORGINA KING LEWIS

KENNIKAT PRESS
Port Washington, N. Y./London

JOHN GREENLEAF WHITTIER

First published in 1913
Reissued in 1972 by Kennikat Press
Library of Congress Catalog Card No: 70-160767
ISBN 0-8046-1589-6

Manufactured by Taylor Publishing Company   Dallas, Texas

TO
ELIZABETH FOSTER BROWN,
WHOM I HONOUR.

ILLUSTRATIONS

	PAGE
Photogravure Portrait of John G. Whittier - - *Frontispiece*	
The Old Homestead at Haverhill -	16
The Interior of the Kitchen at the Homestead - - - -	80
"Snowbound"; the Homestead in Winter - - - - -	148

INTRODUCTION.

IN writing this short life of John Greenleaf Whittier, at the request of my publishers, I have had to draw my information from a great variety of existing publications. There are very numerous Lives, Lectures, Essays, Appreciations, Articles, etc., which have come under my notice and of which I have availed myself freely. From them I have gathered all my limited space would allow.

The life by Samuel T. Pickard in two volumes, has been my authority, since Whittier himself helped so largely in collecting information for all future biographers. I have followed his dates so far as I could ascertain them.

The question whether such a life as I have been able to write is called for, I must leave with those who asked me to undertake the work. But I am confident that the consideration of Whittier's nobility of character, his courage, self-sacrifice, and beautiful spirit in connection with all he undertook, should inspire many hearts to cultivate more of that faithful adherence to Truth so conspicuous in the poet. If my work fails in this it will be due to the portrayal of my hero, not to the hero himself.

I believe that J. G. Whittier's life and work is not known in this country as it deserves to be, and I am hopeful that my sketch may lead to a deeper appreciation of his poems.

To my American friends I feel a word of apology is due for my writing of Whittier without having visited their great Continent. This has not been possible owing to pressure of work, and I must ask them to allow my love for their poet, and for the American people, to overshadow the blemishes that I fear they may discover.

I have endeavoured to portray what manner of man Whittier was ; his poetic genius, the way in which he met difficulties, financial and otherwise, the sacrifice he made for those whom he loved, the abandonment of all ambition for the cause of freedom, and the genuine humility and sense of humour which sweetened all his years.

As a Quaker, he believed in the Divine Immanence. He believed that God's voice can be heard in all hearts who will be obedient, and *his obedience* produced *his life*.

The curse of slavery has not ceased. In my closing chapter I state facts which show that the rights of liberty and justice are withheld from many down-trodden people. Unspeakable cruelties exist, and we are not as a nation keeping our solemn pledges on behalf of the coloured races. If Whittier's life can encourage a "sturdy hate of wrong," a fine sense of right, pity for the oppressed, and a determination to carry on a strong opposition to all unrighteousness, we shall each have to do our part to abolish everything in the nature of slavery everywhere.

I wish to acknowledge my debt of gratitude to all authors whom I have consulted, L. Pickard, G. R. Carpenter, Bliss Perry, F. A. Underwood, my friend W. Garrett Horder, Frances Cooke, and Mrs. Abby Woodman for having furnished me with valuable information.

I am greatly indebted to the Librarian, Norman Penney, and his assistants at

Devonshire House,* who have been most kind in loaning me books, and articles, etc. in old periodicals, and in other ways having come to my aid.

To Elizabeth Foster Brown I wish to express my thanks for suggestions and kind help with the proofs, and Index.

Nor must I fail to mention one nearer home, who has given me the encouragement and assistance that has made my work a pleasure.

Croydon,
    1 mo. 1913.

---

* The Friends' Reference Library.

CHAPTER I

JOHN GREENLEAF WHITTIER'S great-great-grandfather, Thomas Whittier, sailed from Southampton in the spring of the year 1638 for America, to make a home for himself in the West.

In many a Puritan household at that time, thoughts were fixed on a settlement in North America, for they dreamed of religious rights and of liberty, and, as Canning said, they "turned to the new world to redress the balance of the old." The bulk of the emigrants were God-fearing farmers. The grants of land, the reports of a beautiful country and fine climate, were looked upon as a Providential call,* and Thomas Whittier at the age of eighteen, accompanied by two of his uncles and a distant relative, Ruth Green, not doubtless without a wrench, tore himself away from

* Green, "History of the English People," Vol. III., p. 169.

his English home to undertake what was then an adventurous journey to a far country.

A grant of land of considerable dimensions was bestowed upon Thomas soon after his arrival. The river Merrimac flowed through it, and " wooded knolls that ridged the west " were included in the gift. Upon this grant of land in Salisbury, Massachusetts, he built himself a log house. He sought and obtained the consent of Ruth Green, his former travelling companion, to be his wife; for nearly fifty years this dwelling became their home, and it was there that nine children were born to them—five sons, and four daughters.

This ancestor, it is said, was of Huguenot descent, which is quite probable; and certainly John Greenleaf exhibited many Huguenot characteristics, but they may have come through his grandmother, as we shall see later on.

The emigrants who went over to America were men of high moral courage, of religious principle, not easily daunted by the difficulties they met with. The movement headed by George Fox had not begun when Thomas left the old country, but the teaching of the Quakers in after years attracted him, for he did much to secure toleration for the followers of Fox, and his son Joseph, it is known, became a member of the Society of Friends.

During the first forty years of Thomas Whittier's residence in Haverhill, he experienced no trouble with the Indians. They fished and hunted in the vicinity of his home, and they lived on the most friendly terms with the family. Thomas won their respect through the justice he displayed in all his dealings with them, just as William Penn did, who taught the Indians that no advantage was to be taken on either side, and all was to be in love.

But as fresh settlers, not imbued with the same spirit, came thronging into this settlement of peace, and were eager to acquire new land even through unjust measures, the Indians became gradually alienated and hostile, so much so that it was necessary to garrison some of the houses, and Thomas was appointed to select those which were to be places of refuge. Some of the inhabitants were killed, some were carried away captive, but Thomas had no fear, and did not even trouble to bolt his doors at night.

No anxiety was felt when a swarthy, painted face appeared at the window after nightfall: a beautiful illustration of the principle "blessed are the merciful, for they shall obtain mercy."

About the year 1688 Thomas decided to build himself a house which would more conveniently accommodate himself and his large family, and be handed down to his descendants; and his dwelling became the "Whittier Homestead" which the poet has immortalized in "Snowbound."

A picturesque spot was selected for the site upon which a substantial building was reared. The large oaken beams of fifteen inches in width, dear to English hearts, still support the dwelling with its rooms clustering round the central kitchen, which in those days was the most distinguished portion of a farm house. This room was thirty feet long, and proportionately wide. The chimney corner was nearly as large as some of our present day diminutive kitchens, and into it the family could gather on a winter's evening round the crackling wood-fire.

> What matter how the night behaved?
> What matter how the north-wind raved?

THE OLD HOMESTEAD AT HAVERHILL.

Blow high, blow low, not all its snow
Could quench our hearth-fire's ruddy glow,*

wrote the poet years after when memory brought back that cosy corner.

In 1696, Thomas Whittier died. His youngest son had been married a few years before to Mary Peasley, granddaughter of Joseph Peasley, the leading Quaker in the town, through whom the poet's lineage is traced. In 1710, on the death of Thomas's widow the estate was divided among the children, Joseph buying his brothers' and sisters' shares.

Joseph left a large family. The youngest, named after his father, married Sarah Greenleaf in 1730. Whittier the poet has commemorated the home-coming of his grandfather and grandmother in the following lines:

Sarah Greenleaf, of eighteen years,
  Stepped lightly her bridegroom's boat within,
Waving mid-river, through smiles and tears,
  A farewell back to her kith and kin.
With her sweet blue eyes, and her new gold gown,
She sat by her stalwart lover's side—

* "Snowbound."

> Oh, never was brought to Haverhill town
>   By land or water so fair a bride.
> Glad at the glad autumnal weather,
>   The Indian summer so soft and warm,
> They walked through the golden woods together,
>   His arm the girdle about her form.*

Joseph and Sarah had eleven children, only three of whom married. John, the youngest, was father to the poet. At the age of forty-four, he married Abigail Hussey, who was twenty-one years his junior. They had four children, Mary, John Greenleaf, Matthew, and Elizabeth.

John Greenleaf Whittier was born December 17th, 1807.

Some doubt has been thrown on Whittier's being descended from the Huguenots; but he himself has said that the Greenleaf family were Huguenots who left France on account of their religious principles and settled in England in the course of the sixteenth century. The name was probably translated from the French, the Acadians, he says, having a habit of changing their names for the English equivalent; thus Feuillevert became Green-

---
* "The Home-coming of the Bride."

leaf. It seems very probable that his natural refinement and striking appearance, far removed from the farmer type of father and uncles, was an inheritance he gained through his grandmother.

Farmer Whittier was an honest, worthy man, much respected in his neighbourhood. He was by birthright and conviction a Friend, and every First-day he and his family drove in the old-fashioned chaise to Meeting at Amesbury, eight miles off. The homestead at Haverhill was isolated from the neighbouring dwellings. The country was well wooded, but on the south green meadows stretched far away, and the brook, after its falls through the ravine, rushed over the boulders to the larger stream which flowed into the river, doing service as it travelled along by turning the wheels of two or three saw and grist mills. From the summit of Job's Hill a very fine view was obtained of the woods and the Lake Henoza, and when the wind was in a certain quarter the waves could be heard breaking over Salisbury beach.

In trying to picture this happy homestead we are greatly helped by the vivid description given by the poet when, left alone in his old age to mourn the death of his beloved sister Elizabeth, he consoled himself by calling up the scenes of early days, when snowbound in the old home, with few books and no magazines, the necessary resource of telling stories was resorted to during the long winter evenings.

The family consisted of father, mother, uncle, aunt, two sons, and two daughters, the schoolmaster who took up his abode with the family for the greater part of the year, and in addition, Harriet Livermore, the "not unfeared, half-welcome guest."

The father was a "prompt, decisive" man, never wasting unnecessary words, interested in town affairs, and often called in to settle disputes, owing to his character for justice. In dealing with charities his maxim was expressed in the following words: "There are the Lord's poor, and the Devil's poor; there ought to be a distinction made between them by the overseers of the poor." From his children he expected, and received, obedience, the good old-fashioned way of cultivating reverence; and in thinking of him his son recalls the love that bound them together and lived on when earthly vision had long vanished and the voice was still, as his heart warmed at the thought that "love can never lose its own."

The kind and tenderly-loving mother was esteemed by those who knew her as one of the loveliest and saintliest of women, "elevating almost into religious rites the whiteness of her bread and the purity of her table linen." For fifty years she was the guide and counsellor of her son. She would sit in her chimney corner turning her spinning wheel, as she related

> How the Indian hordes came down
> At midnight on Cocheco town,
> And how her own great-uncle bore
> His cruel scalp-mark to fourscore.
> Recalling, in her fitting phrase,
>   So rich and picturesque and free,
>   (The common unrhymed poetry
> Of simple life and country ways,)
> The story of her early days.*

Near by the mother sat Aunt Mercy,

> The sweetest woman ever Fate
> Perverse denied a household mate,
> Who, lonely, homeless, not the less
> Found peace in love's unselfishness.*

* "Snowbound."

But she had had her romance. When young she was betrothed to an attractive young man worthy of her affections. One night, as she mused by the fire in the big kitchen after the family had retired to rest, she thought she heard a sound, and, on looking out of the window, she saw her lover riding past. She hastened to the front door, passing as she went the porch window. Again she saw him, but on opening the door all was quiet and no one was in sight. Terrified, for the vision had been so real, she went to her sister, who tried to soothe her, "Thee has been dreaming by the fire, Mercy," she said, and urged her to go to bed; but Mercy knew she had not been dreaming, and after many weary days, news came to her from a strange hand, that her lover had died on the day, and at the time, when she saw the vision.

Then there was the uncle, " innocent of books, rich in lore of fields and brooks," a man after a boy's heart, full of stories of the " feats on pond and river done,"

> Till, warming with the tales he told,
> Forgotten was the outside cold.

Greenleaf had two sisters and one brother.

Of the two sisters, Mary was most like her father, and Elizabeth, the life-long companion of her brother, possessed the sweeter nature of the mother.

Elizabeth was his special pet and became his literary friend and adviser in after years. Her life was one of unselfish devotion to her brother, who speaks of her "dark eyes full of love's content." When she had entered within the veil, he writes of her thus:

And yet, dear heart! remembering thee,
  Am I not richer than of old?
Safe in thy immortality,
  What change can reach the wealth I hold?
  What chance can mar the pearl and gold
Thy love hath left in trust with me?*

The schoolmaster, George Haskell, who lodged with the Whittiers, was a happy addition to the company. He was musical and delighted the young people, though he was a man of the old school, believing in the cane.

Brisk wielder of the birch and rule,*

but withal full of fun and frolic, singing to his fiddle, or playing with the boys, courteous

* "Snowbound."

to the women folk, patient and unselfish, so that Whittier says of him,

> Happy the snow-locked homes wherein
> He tuned his merry violin.*

But there was one guest whom the Whittiers generously housed, perchance with the thought that such unity and happiness should be shared by one—

> Presaging ill to him, whom Fate
> Condemned to share her love, or hate.*

Harriet Livermore was a person whose wanderings occasionally took her to Haverhill, and Whittier, when a boy, dreaded her arrival, though in later years he did much to befriend her. She possessed a very violent temper and had little control over it. Finding the gentle Friends did not call forth her passions as many did, she sought, and obtained, admission into the Society of Friends, but on getting into an argument on some doctrinal point with a young man, she knocked him down, which made her religious profession doubtful, and her connection with the community was brought to a close.

*"Snowbound."

We can now picture the family party in the large kitchen with its huge fireplace, on a cold winter's night, the wind howling outside, the fire crackling inside, the love binding each to the others, the happiness of contentment, the joy of humorous rivalry, the quiet time of gratitude,

> For food, and shelter, warmth and health,
> And love's contentment more than wealth,*

ere the pleasant circle broke up for the night.

---

* "Snowbound."

CHAPTER II

WHITTIER'S boyhood was spent on the farm, and his occupations were those of a farmer's son, attending to the animals, milking the cows, watching the growth of the crops and harvesting them. His mother made the butter and cheese, both of which were greatly in request and fetched good prices. The uplands which had been cleared of trees were strewn with huge boulders, making the working of the soil heavy and difficult, but the boy did his share and fair crops were the reward. Rye and Indian corn were raised, and the only method of threshing the grain was with the flail, which required more strength than Greenleaf possessed, but he worked hard, and never murmured at the strain on a not over robust constitution.

There is little doubt that the rough life and exposure to the intense cold with insufficient clothing, and the long chilly drives of eight miles to the Meeting House, which was never warmed, contributed largely to the physical suffering which followed the poet through life.

The family held a leading position in the district, and drew around them a circle of refined and cultured people.

Visiting Friends came from time to time, as is the custom in the Society, with words of encouragement and comfort which were highly valued. On First-days as many would drive to Meeting as the chaise would accommodate, and in the afternoon they gathered together, when the Scriptures, or such books as they possessed, were read. There was no lack of interest or comment, and the heroes of the Old Testament were freely criticised. On one occasion young Greenleaf questioned if King David with his war-like propensities could have been received into the Society of Friends. This seems to have occasioned some difficulty, and as it was not easy to escape the battle scenes of the Old Testament, the parents turned their attention more exclusively to the New.

In looking back upon those early days, Whittier speaks of the interest he felt in the changing seasons, in dreaming of " something wonderful and grand, somewhere in the future, of losing nothing, and gaining much," of his thirst for knowledge, and the impression made upon him of holy lives, leaving him with a sense of "falling short, and longing for a better state."

The little school-house to which he and his sister Mary went, was about half a mile from their house, and there they used to trudge, to and fro, whenever they could be spared from the farm. The teaching must have been of a very primitive nature, but Greenleaf had a retentive memory and what he learned he made his own, always eager for fresh knowledge of the outside world. On every available occasion the boy, pencil in hand, would scribble on any piece of paper or wood he could obtain for the purpose. The quick insight of a mother's heart guessed something of what was passing in the boy's mind, and she sewed some sheets of paper together for him that he might comfort himself by writing down his thoughts upon them.

One pretty little incident was either noted down on those pages, or treasured in the boy's heart, of a day at school, when a little girl lingered behind and sweetly apologized for having taken his place at the top of the class. We extract the story from "In School-days." After describing the school-house, he says:

> Long years ago a winter sun
>   Shone over it at setting;
> Lit up its western window-panes,
>   And low eaves' icy fretting.
>
> It touched the tangled golden curls,
>   And brown eyes full of grieving,
> Of one who still her steps delayed
>   When all the school were leaving.
>
> For near her stood the little boy
>   Her childish favor singled:
> His cap pulled low upon a face
>   Where pride and shame were mingled.
>
> Pushing with restless feet the snow
>   To right and left, he lingered;—
> As restlessly her tiny hands
>   The blue-checked apron fingered.
>
> He saw her lift her eyes; he felt
>   The soft hand's light caressing,
> And heard the tremble of her voice,
>   As if a fault confessing.
>
> "I'm sorry that I spelt the word:
>   I hate to go above you,
> Because,"—the brown eyes lower fell,—
>   "Because, you see, I love you!"

> Still memory to a gray-haired man
>   That sweet child-face is showing.
> Dear girl! the grasses on her grave
>   Have forty years been growing!
>
> He lives to learn, in life's hard school,
>   How few who pass above him
> Lament their triumph and his loss,
>   Like her,—because they love him.

When Whittier was about fourteen years of age, Joshua Coffin came as a teacher to the Haverhill district. He was wont to spend many of his evenings with the Whittier family, and brought books of history and travel, which he read aloud to the little company when the day's work was done. This was a new interest for Greenleaf, and of all the listeners he was the most eager to gain every advantage from the fresh knowledge of the world opening out to him. One evening Joshua Coffin brought a volume of Burns' poems, and read one after another to the family. On raising his eyes now and again he was struck with the look on Greenleaf's face. The boy was spellbound, and seemed lost to all but his own conflicting thoughts. Before retiring for the night Coffin handed the volume to the lad to study at his leisure.

This was Greenleaf's first insight into true poetry, and he always realized that he owed a debt to Burns, which he acknowledged, many years later, in one of the finest tributes to the poet that has been written :—

> Sweet day, sweet songs ! the golden hours
>   Grew brighter for that singing,
> From brook and bird and meadow flowers
>   A dearer welcome bringing.
>
> New light on home-seen Nature beamed,
>   New glory over Woman ;
> And daily life and duty seemed
>   No longer poor and common.

Thus he remembered the new world into which Burns introduced him, and nothing is more touching than his reference to the great poet's violation of the moral laws.

> Let those who never erred forget
>   His worth, in vain bewailings ;
> Sweet Soul of Song ! I own my debt
>   Uncancelled by his failings !
>
> Lament who will the ribald line
>   Which tells his lapse from duty,
> How kissed the maddening lips of wine
>   Or wanton ones of beauty;

> But think, while falls that shade between
>   The erring one and Heaven,
> That he who loved like Magdalen,
>   Like her may be forgiven.*

Greenleaf was incited through his admiration for Burns to try to make his own verses. He wrote of that period:

> I found that the things out of which poems came were not, as I had always imagined, somewhere far off in a world of life lying outside our own sky. They were right here about my feet and among the people I knew.

His slate was now covered with rhymes, and when the farm day's work was over he hid himself in an unoccupied upper chamber, safe, as he thought, from all human eyes, and there he wrote many of his early effusions, of which very little remains. He made a rhymed catalogue of the few books in the house, the contents of which he had almost committed to memory, and in these crude efforts we see the boy's passionate desire for some higher education. The father had little or no sympathy with what he regarded as a foolish waste of time, but as the boy did his work well he left him to spend his spare moments as he pleased. His mother and sister Mary

* "Burns."

guessed where the boy's heart was, and were ever sympathetic. Instead of being seen, as before, when work was over, by the river bank or on Job's Hill, he would climb the attic stair and disappear for hours.

Mary's curiosity was excited. She wanted to see what was the result of all those quiet hours, and one day when Greenleaf was in the fields, she crept upstairs and soon found his treasures. Sitting on the floor she read and read, till her heart burned within her and her face flushed at the discovery that her brother was a poet. With sisterly pride, and no thought of asking leave, she picked out the poem she judged the best, and with much care and difficulty made a copy of it, which she sent off to the editor of the *Free Press*.

William Lloyd Garrison had lately started a weekly paper, and its liberal and benevolent sympathies so pleased John Whittier that he subscribed for it. In the *Free Press* there was a Poet's Corner, and Mary thought her selection of "The Exile's Departure" was quite equal to some of the verses she had read in the paper. She sent it anonymously, only stating the age of the writer.

The postman's arrival was an event eagerly looked forward to week by week, and the Poet's Corner was of special interest to Greenleaf. One day, as he was helping his father mend a stone wall that ran by the side of the road, he heard the familiar and welcome trot of the postman's pony, and on looking up, a copy of the *Free Press* was tossed to him. He soon opened it and turned at once, as was his wont, to the corner of special interest. There, to his astonishment, he read " The Exile's Departure "—his own composition, hidden away as he thought in his sacred attic. Underneath the poem he read the following paragraph :

The author of this sketch, which would do credit to riper years, is a youth of sixteen, who we think bids fair to prove another Bernard Barton of whose persuasion he is. His poetry bears the stamp of true poetic genius, which if carefully cultivated will rank him among the bards of his country.

His father's voice brought him to himself, the paper fell to his feet, he took up his trowel and continued to place the heavy stones one upon another.

All who remember seeing their thoughts in print for the first time will understand the thrill of joy, not unmixed with a sense of fear, which passed through young Greenleaf's mind as he realized that he had been launched upon the sea of literature and was a public character.

After the excitement was over he decided to send another poem, "The Deity," to the editor. That too was accepted, and W. L. Garrison determined to seek an interview with the writer. He was little older than Greenleaf, and had started very early in life at editorial work. His father had deserted his wife and family, and Lloyd when quite a lad, had begun to earn his own living, though of school days he had known but little. He had been taken as an apprentice by a printer, and made the most of every opportunity that opened to him. Hearing, through enquiry from the postman, the direction from which the Haverhill letters came, Garrison drove out some fourteen miles one day to discover his promising young contributor.

Whittier was in the field when Mary went forth to tell him of the arrival of W. L. Garrison, and to persuade him to return to the house with her. The boy was shy, and it was with some difficulty she induced him to face the ordeal.

Garrison, with his natural, gracious manner, soon put Greenleaf at his ease, complimented him on his work, assured him of future success, and, on the appearance of his father, strongly advised the boy's having some educational advantages. Mr. Whittier was not pleased at this suggestion, and he said, "Poetry will never give him bread, and such foolish notions had better be set aside."

In writing to Garrison years after this meeting, Greenleaf in his loyalty to his father's memory said: "My father did not oppose me, he was proud of my pieces, but he was in straitened circumstances and could do nothing for me. But he was a man in advance of his time and free from popular errors of thinking."

How much of future good was to evolve from that first meeting of the two youths; each destined to take a leading part in his country's welfare; each to suffer, each to fight, each to grasp great and abiding principles, and work them out. It was impossible that life could be the same to the lad after this day of excitement. He went back to his farm work, but fresh hopes, and great longings were stirred, which could never be again stifled.

Circumstances shortly after made it necessary for Garrison to remove to Boston, which induced Whittier to offer his verses to the *Haverhill Gazette*. Mr. Thayer, the editor, appreciating the latent talent in the boy, visited the farm, as Garrison had done, and pleaded that Greenleaf might attend a new Academy soon to be opened in Haverhill. With this suggestion he offered to board the boy for six months if the farmer could pay the fees. Mr. Whittier had been realising that the farm work was too heavy for his son, and had been anxious about his health, so, after talking over the whole matter with his wife, he told Greenleaf he would raise no difficulties, but owing to the mortgage on the farm, he was unable to aid him in paying the fees. If in any way he could earn the money, he was free to go.

Nothing now stood between Greenleaf and the accomplishment of his secret ambition but the lack of money. How to earn it was the problem he had to solve.

The country people of Haverhill who worked on their farms through the summer had little to do through the winter months, so to earn a little money, and occupy the time, they followed some trade, such as that of a wheelwright, or shoemaker. It soon became known that Greenleaf had received an offer to attend the Academy and was full of eagerness to earn the school fees. One farmer who made shoes in the winter offered to teach him the art, which offer was accepted with genuine delight, and the simple slippers were soon turned out by the boy, who knew the value of every cent he was laying by. He received eight cents for each pair, but so fast and eagerly did he work that during the first winter he earned enough to pay for six months training at the Academy.

He calculated that he had made enough to have twenty-five cents in his pocket at the close of the term, and so it proved. His habit was never to buy anything till he had the money to pay for it, and though for many years his income was very small he was never in debt.

A boy of such grit and principle was sure to succeed. A story is told of how when bidden at his first school to recite the Westminster Confession he refused. When asked the reason, "Father says I must not because it isn't true." A whipping was threatened, but quietly and firmly the lad answered, "Thee can whip me, but thee can never make me say it." Of such stuff the saints and martyrs are made, not with aggressive force but with immovable determination.

On May 1st, 1827, Whittier began his higher education at the Haverhill Academy. His entrance at the opening of the Institution is memorable for the ode composed by the boy for the occasion, and sung with no little pride by the future scholars. Unfortunately no copy of this has been preserved. Mr. Thayer's kind and generous suggestion was carried out, and Whittier lived with his family, and was able to indulge his literary taste by reading many standard works to be found in the editor's large library. Greenleaf was quite conscious of the great kindness shown him, and refers to it years after, when writing to Mr. Thayer's son : " I never think of thy mother without feelings of love and gratitude. She and thy father were my best friends in the hard struggle of my schooldays."

We have a vivid picture of the youth, as he was at that time, in a sketch of him by Judge Minot's daughter. " He was nearly nineteen years old when I first saw him. He was a very handsome, distinguished-looking young man. His eyes were remarkably beautiful. He was tall, slight, and very erect ; a bashful youth but never awkward, my mother says, who was a better judge than I. Whittier was always kind to children, and under a very grave and quiet exterior there was a real love of fun and a keen sense of the ludicrous. With intimate friends he talked a great deal, and in a wonderfully interesting manner ; usually earnest, often analytical, and frequently playful. When a wrong was to be righted, or an evil to be remedied, he was readier to act than any young man I ever knew, and was very wise in his action, shrewd, sensible, practical. I think it was always his endeavour

> to render less
> The sum of human wretchedness."

As the six months passed Whittier began to question how he was going to earn the needed money for his next term at the Academy. A schoolmaster was required in a neighbouring village, and when it was known that Whittier was seeking for work the post was offered to him. He gladly accepted it, and with the money earned by teaching, and posting up the ledgers of a storekeeper, he attended the second term, graduated, and returned home to farm work again.

CHAPTER III

WILLIAM LLOYD GARRISON had lost touch with Whittier, but he had not forgotten him. On hearing how he had earned enough money to pay his school fees, of his success at the Academy, and that he had graduated and gone back to farm work, he bestirred himself to see what could be done for so promising a youth.

Garrison was editing *The Philanthropist*, a weekly paper devoted largely to the Temperance cause—the first paper of the kind ever published. He thought Whittier might relieve him of the editorship, while he devoted himself to wider fields of usefulness in reforms which his publishers did not patronize.

On making this suggestion to W. and W. Collier, they sent a letter to Whittier offering him the editorship of their paper.

Whittier was much exercised in his mind as to what answer to make, and turned to his kind friend Mr. Thayer for advice.

28th of 11 mo., 1828.

Friend A. W. Thayer,

I have been in a quandary ever since I left thee, whether I had better accept the offer of Friend Collier, or *nail* myself down to my seat, —for verily I could not be kept there otherwise —and toil for the honorable and truly gratifying distinction of being considered " a good cobbler.". . . No, no, friend, it won't do. Thee might as well catch a weasel asleep, or the old enemy of mankind in a parsonage-house, as find me contented with that distinction.

I have renounced college for the good reason that I have no disposition to humble myself to meanness for an education—crowding myself through upon the charities of others, and leaving it with a debt, or an obligation, to weigh down my spirit like an incubus, and paralyze every exertion. The professions are already crowded full to overflowing ; and I, forsooth, because I have a miserable knack of rhyming, must swell the already enormous number, struggle awhile with debt and difficulties, and then, weary of life, go down to my original insignificance, where the tinsel of classical honors will but aggravate my misfortune. Verily, friend Thayer, the picture is a dark one, but from my heart I believe it to be true. What, then, remains for me ? School-keeping—out upon it ! The memory of last year's experience comes up before me like a horrible dream. No, I had rather be a tin peddlar. Seriously, the situation of editor of *The Philanthropist* is not only respectable, but it is peculiarly pleasant to one who takes so deep an interest, as I really do, in the great cause it is laboring to promote. I would rather have the memory of a Howard, a Wilberforce, and a Clarkson, than the undying fame of Byron. I have written to friend Collier but have entered into no engagement. I should like to see or hear from Mr. Carlton [the Principal of the Academy] before I do anything. He is one of the best men—to use a phrase of *my craft*—that ever trod shoe leather.

Whittier decided to accept the offer made him, and at the beginning of the year 1828, he left home to enter the printing office of the Colliers in Boston. The senior partner of the firm was a Baptist minister, with whom Whittier resided. One of the papers published by the firm was the *American Manufacturer*, a political journal which week by week contained a poem by Whittier, and his support of the paper won him considerable popularity.

To Mr. Thayer he writes :—

The *Manufacturer* goes down, thanks to the gullibility of the public, and we are doing very well. Have had one or two rubs with other papers, but I have had some compliments which were quite as much as my sanity could swallow.

Garrison could not have had a more sympathetic follower to don his mantle than young Whittier, for he had said of the paper when writing to his friend :

I admire your plan of directing your efforts against those fearful evils—slavery, intemperance and war. Heart and hand I unite with you in denouncing them. It shall be my endeavor to merit that name which I consider of all others the most worthy of our ambition—the friend of man.

In the following year Whittier was unfortunately called home on account of the failing health of his father. His uncle was dead, his brother had left the farm, and his father was not able to attend to the work as formerly. Whittier, ever thinking of the interests of others rather than of his own, gave up his position in the printing office without hesitation, and once again started ploughing, and digging, and planning to raise money to pay off the mortgage on the farm. He had saved out of his salary a sum of money for this purpose.

But he had gained more than a salary when in Boston, for he had had opportunities of access to good libraries, and after settling down again in the old home he spent his evenings in writing for various publications, in editing the *Haverhill Gazette*, and in study. As his poems were circulated he received many complimentary expressions of approval, but hardly any of his writings at that time have been preserved.

In 1830 his father died, and Whittier was left in charge of his mother and sister. The hard work on the farm began again to tell on his health. It was evident that he was not physically strong enough for it, but he made no complaint, and even the dear sister Elizabeth, his life-long friend and companion, failed to realize the strain upon his constitution.

An opening came, however, to relieve him. The editor of the *New England Review*, having to leave Connecticut for a time, looked round for someone to fill his place. This was the chief paper in the State, and had the largest circulation. The editor had no knowledge that Whittier was only three and twenty years of age, so wrote offering him the post with a good salary. Whittier, in later years, said, "If I had heard I had been appointed Prime Minister to the Khan of Tartary, I should not have been more astonished."

It was no easy matter to make up his mind as to his duty. He felt he was wanted on the farm, and he had had little experience of political life, though so keenly interested in it, and he was not unconscious of his limitations. He lay awake all night, and in the morning laid the matter before his mother and sister, leaving the decision in their hands. His mother advised him to undertake it, so, after making arrangements for the farm, he once more left the home and undertook the work assigned him at Hartford.

It was an exciting time. The leading politicians were preparing for the coming election of a President for the United States.

Young Whittier's predecessor had introduced him in his paper in the following glowing terms :—

I cannot do less than congratulate my readers on the prospect of their more familiar acquaintance with a gentleman of such powerful energies, and such exalted purity and sweetness of character. I have made some enemies among those whose good opinion I value, but no rational man can ever be the enemy of Mr. Whittier.

Great interest was felt in the prospect of meeting this exceptional individual, and what was the dismay among his first visitors on finding a homely youth in Quaker homespun clothes, very quiet, and not too ready of speech. For a short time there was considerable perturbation as to what they should do, but ere long they discovered in Whittier a strength of character, and a courage to stand by his principles, that gained their admiration and respect.

Of course his political opponents scoffed at anything they could find, or invent, to scoff at, as is the manner of opponents; and one day on opening a paper Whittier saw a long article under the heading " John Greenleaf Whittier." It was an abusive and offensive attack on his work as editor. He kept the matter to himself, but with a heavy heart; and after a time he wrote to the author, asking for fair play. For answer he received a letter of derision at his being so thin-skinned. He laid it away, saying nothing about it.

He plodded on, throwing his whole energy

into the struggle his country was passing through, and soon began to earn friendly notice, and receive much encouragement and invitations to visit other editors in New York and Boston.

He wrote the political leaders, many sketches, legends, stories, and poems. Also at this time he collected much that he had written, and brought out his first book, which he called " Legends of New England in Prose and Verse."

Few, if any, copies of this work exist, and his suppression of them afterwards shows him to have judged his own powers fairly correctly. When the author, in later years, came across any of the volumes he destroyed them, and on one occasion he paid five dollars that he might have the satisfaction of burning a copy, confessing he could hardly believe it was his own composition.

But the first sign of his greatness was manifest in his early years, and is to be seen in " The Song of the Vermonters," written during his schooldays, and published anonymously. Dr. Carpenter, a keen critic, speaks of that poem as " of real excellence." The secret of the authorship, however, was not discovered for sixty years.

In the March of 1831, Whittier was again called home to help his mother in settling the business connected with his father's estate. He had saved enough money to pay off the mortgage on the farm but his presence was needed, yet he had ties with Hartford, where he resided for some months when editing the *Review*, and was, as he says, "driven from pillar to post."

The anxiety prostrated him, he was obliged to give up his editorial work on the *Review*, and in October we find him under a doctor's care, "pledged to return him hale and breathing, or with his bones neatly done up in his travelling trunk."

To Jonathan Law, formerly postmaster of Hartford, with whom Whittier had boarded, he shows his disappointment in not having been able to get back to Hartford, and says:

I have been at home all the time, half sick, half mad. Now you will suppose I have got the 'hypo.' No such thing. It is as real as the nose on my face, this illness of mine—alas too real. Nor am I under the cerulean influence of the blue devils *now*,—the last blue-visaged imp has departed with my exorcism in his ears... Now don't imagine for one moment that

I have become morose and melancholy. Far from it. I am among anxious friends. I have a thousand sources of enjoyment even in the midst of corporeal suffering. I have excellent Society here to visit, and receive visits from. The girls here are nice specimens of what girls should be. You will find a description of one or two of them in a poem which I shall send you in a few weeks, a poem partly written at your house and which is being published. It lay around in fragments staring me everywhere in the face and at last to get rid of it I have given it over to the bookmakers. They will have a hard bargain with it.

From this time on he struggled against continued weakness, suffering much with headache and sleeplessness as well as an affection of the heart, the doctors always warning him against undue excitement. To write steadily for an hour more often than not resulted in severe pain in his head. Happily, however, his humorous nature enabled him not only to keep cheerful himself when unable to work, but to enliven many an evening with his jokes. One has been preserved in which he made his mother his victim.

Ministering Friends, when attending the

Monthly and Quarterly Meetings in connection with the Society of Friends, were often entertained at Whittier's house. On one occasion Sophronia Page had been staying with the family, and, on leaving in the early morning when not very light, she put on Mrs. Whittier's bonnet by mistake. The Quaker bonnets in those days were all alike, so to avoid such an exchange the name of the owner was written in the crown. Owing to the darkness of the morning Sophronia Page missed the mark.

On reaching home she saw what she had done, and immediately returned the bonnet with a note of apology to Greenleaf, trusting him to smooth the way for it to be returned to his mother.

The temptation, however, to a bit of fun was too strong within him to be resisted.

He left the band-box in the hall and went and seated himself by the side of his mother, appearing in great distress of mind.

His mother was at once anxious to know what was amiss.

"Why, Greenleaf," she said, "what is the matter? Is thee ill?"

"No, I am not ill," he replied, "but I am very sad and troubled."

"Tell me what has happened," she cried.

"Mother, it will shock and grieve thee so, it will make thee sick at heart."

The poor lady's excitement increased— "Don't keep me in suspense, my boy, tell me the worst at once."

With apparent enforced calmness Greenleaf said, "Mother, has thee heard from Sophronia Page since she left here?"

"Why, no, no, has anything happened to her, is she sick?"

"She is not sick," he replied, "and no ordinary thing has happened to her. There is something terrible coming out against her; it will shake the Yearly Meeting."

"What is thee talking about? I believe Sophronia Page is too well balanced to take any rash step in the Society troubles. Don't keep me waiting."

"Well, Mother, if thee will know I must tell thee. Sophronia Page, incredible as it may seem, has been taking what does not belong to her."

At this his mother's indignation was aroused, and she replied, "Greenleaf, I'd have thee know that Sophronia Page is not a woman to make light jokes about. I don't see any fun in such talk."

To which he gravely replied: "Mother, this is no idle joke; I am telling the truth. Sophronia Page has been taking what does not belong to her. Thee will have to believe it, for she has begun to restore what she has taken!"

He then produced the bonnet, and his mother said, "Greenleaf, if thee were twenty years younger I would take thee over my knee!"

Through the winter of 1832 Whittier was hardly able to do any work through ill-health. He wrote to Mrs. Sigourney, who had often contributed to his paper and had shown him much kindness:

I have scarcely done anything this winter. There have been few days in which I have been able to write with any degree of comfort. I have indeed thrown together a poem of some length, the title of which, "Moll Pitcher," has very little connection with the subject. This poem I handed to a friend of mine, and he has threatened to publish it. If I thought I deserved half the compliments you have been pleased to bestow upon my humble exertions I should certainly be in danger of becoming obnoxious to the charge of vanity. The truth is I love poetry with a love as warm, as fervent, as sincere, as any of the more gifted worshippers at the temple of the Muses. But I feel and know that

> " To other chords than mine belong
> The breathing of immortal song."

And in consequence I have been compelled to trust to other and less pleasant pursuits for distinction and profit. Politics is the only field now open for me and there is something inconsistent in the character of a poet and a modern politician.

"Moll Pitcher" was suppressed by Whittier after a revised edition, and has never been published in any collection of his works. He sent several contributions to different magazines, but in another communication to Mrs. Sigourney he indicates that politics were laying hold of him.

He was a Christian before he was a poet, and his interest in his fellow creatures was leading him to say

> Self-ease is pain ; the only rest
> Is labour for a worthy end.*

Thus he felt that he must exercise all his energies to redress the wrongs of humanity

* " The Voices."

and stay the hand of war. "Of poetry," he says, "I have nearly taken my leave, and a pen is getting to be something of a stranger to me. I have been compelled again to plunge into the political whirlpool, for I have found that my political reputation is more influential than my poetical, so I try to make myself a man of the world, and the public are deceived, but I am not. They do not see that I have thrown the rough armour of rude and turbulent controversy over a keenly sensitive bosom—a heart of softer and gentler emotions than I dare expose."

He was passing through a time of great strain, and there is little doubt that the "softer and gentler emotions" were being strongly moved through keen disappointment, and the "half sick, half mad" condition of which he spoke to his friend, Jonathan Law, was the result of a disappointment in love. The following letter to Miss Russ, daughter of Judge Russ, did not receive the answer he hoped for; and with his sensitive and affectionate nature, which sought the sympathy and companionship of women, we can understand that for a time he was distraught with ill-health, the uncertainty of his financial position, the questionable joy of being a public character, and the consciousness of unrequited love.

Miss Russ,—I could not leave town without asking an interview with you. I know that my proposal is abrupt, and I cannot but fear that it will be unwelcome. But you will pardon me. About to leave Hartford for a distant part of the country, I have ventured to make a demand for which, under any other circumstances, I should be justly censurable. I feel that I have indeed no claims on your regard. But I would hope, almost against any evidence to the contrary, that you might not altogether discourage a feeling which has long been to me as a new existence. I would hope that in my absence from my own New England, whether in the sunny South or the " Far West " one heart would respond with my own, one bright eye grow brighter at the mention of a name which has never been, and I trust never will be, connected with dishonor,—and which, if the Ambition which now urges onward shall continue in vigorous exercise, shall yet be known widely and well, and whose influence shall be lastingly felt.

But this is dreaming,—and it may only call forth a smile. . . . . . I leave town on

Saturday. Can you allow an interview this evening or on that of Friday? If however you cannot consistently afford me the pleasure of seeing you—I have only to resign hopes dear to me as life itself, and carry with me hereafter the curse of disappointed feeling.

A note in answer will be waited for impatiently. At least you will not deny me this,

Yours most truly,
J. G. WHITTIER.*

Thursday afternoon.

---

* *Century Magazine*, May, 1912.

CHAPTER IV.

IT was three years since W. Lloyd Garrison and Whittier had seen each other, but in the meantime Whittier had written a poem for his paper the *Haverhill Gazette*. He knew that Garrison was fighting the iniquitous proposal that the United States should go to war with Mexico in order to obtain the free lands of Texas on which slave states should be formed, and that he was demanding that his countrymen should rise and protest against this scheme.

Garrison wrote strong words against the slave traffic and the cowardice of those who endorsed it. A libel was brought against him by a merchant whom he had accused of carrying slaves in his ship, and, not being able to pay the fine, he was imprisoned.

On hearing this, Whittier urged a wealthy statesman to pay the fine and set Garrison free. A New York merchant, however, stepped in, paid the demand and liberated the politician.

This imprisonment only made Garrison more determined than ever to free his countrymen if possible, and for that purpose he started a little anti-slavery paper, which he named the *Liberator,* and as a heading gave as his motto " Our country is the world—our countrymen are mankind."

There was no concealing his purpose. " Urge me not," he said, " to use moderation in a cause like the present. I am in earnest. I will not equivocate. I will not excuse. I will not retreat a single inch. *And I will be heard."*

The paper made its way North and South. And when the Northern States realised that the mill owners would be ruined, and the men in the Southern States thought their lives would be in danger, if the slaves were set free, large rewards were offered to anyone who would capture Garrison and take him South for trial.

Garrison, thinking of his talks with Whittier, who as a Quaker had inherited a strong sense of the guilt attached to slavery, summoned him to join the army that was fighting for freedom, in the following words :

My brother, there are upwards of two million of our country men who are doomed to the most horrible servitude which ever cursed our race and blackened the page of history. There are one hundred thousand of their offspring kidnapped annually from their birth. The southern portion of our country is going down to destruction, physically and morally, with a swift descent, carrying other portions with her. This, then, is a time for the philanthropist—any friend of his country—to put forth his energies in order to let the oppressed go free, and sustain the republic. The cause is worthy of Gabriel; yea, the God of Hosts places Himself at its head. Whittier, enlist! Your talents, zeal, influence—all are needed.

Garrison had the right to ask a sacrifice from another. He was giving his life for the cause, living in one mean, unfurnished room, in which he did his printing, existing chiefly on bread and water.

Whittier was not the man to refuse such a call, but what did this mean to him? To be one of the despised and hated Anti-Slavery company; to lay aside all ambitions of popularity, deliberately to take up a cross for his fellow man, and to be removed, as he thought, out of the sphere he so much loved.

He did not even hesitate. Again the old truth which never fails bore fruit : "He that loseth his life shall find it." He was giving up what seemed so dear to him, at the call of God, and yet in ways he dreamed not of this very service of sacrifice was the inspiration which made him a genuine poet.

A good critic of his work remarks : "No sooner had he abandoned his dream of personal advancement than the Byronic melancholy, the weak imitations of Scott, and the echoes of Mrs. Felicia Hemans, disappear from his verse. He was studying the prose of Milton and Burke, those organ voices of English liberty. From Burns and Byron he now caught only the passion for justice and the common rights of all. He forgot himself. The cause of negro emancipation in America—to his mind only one phase of the struggle for a wider human freedom everywhere—stirred and deepened his whole nature."*

His first act was to write a pamphlet entitled " Justice and Expediency." It is a powerful appeal. He sweeps away the mockery of expressing " sympathy " for the slaves when there was no readiness

Bliss Perry, p. 21.

to act, for in 1828, when a meeting wa called of all the clergymen in Boston, only eight attended. The "sympathy," Whittier says, "is like artificial flowers of sentiment over imaginable wrong, whitewashing the sepulchre." He holds up to scorn all suggestions short of abolition. He quotes illustration upon illustration to prove that free labour is more productive than forced, and he shows "the legacy of infamy" that must follow *all* slavery.

    Their glory and their might
Shall perish ; and their very names shall be
Vile before all the people, in the light
    Of a world's liberty.*

This pamphlet he published at his own expense with the hard-earned money that he had been saving for years.

Financially he knew he must suffer greatly by joining an unpopular cause, and for some years the struggle was keen, and to keep out of debt and support himself and his family became a constant difficulty. Though Quakers were often tolerated as other heretics were not, Whittier's outspoken trumpet blasts for Freedom exasperated many of his friends. At the same time, the

    " Clerical Oppressors."

often strange paradoxes in human nature led many of them to admire the courage which spoke a truth their own hearts could not deny, though they dared not say so.

The first edition of his pamphlet was soon exhausted, and an extra issue of 5,000 was published and paid for by Lewis Tappan, of New York, a wealthy man and a firm friend to the slaves.

The temper, however, which was manifested in some quarters is seen in the fact that, for lending a copy to his brother, Dr. Reuben Crandall, of Washington, was arrested and sent to prison, being liberated after a time, only to die from the injury to his health caused by cruelty and confinement in a loathsome city jail. This incident Whittier has preserved in the following lines :

> Beside me gloomed the prison-cell
> Where wasted one in slow decline
> For uttering simple words of mine,
> And loving freedom all too well.*

Whittier soon saw he had committed himself to a cause that would not triumph for many a year ; he knew he had lost all hope of political preferment, and, keenest

* "Astræa at the Capitol."

trial of all, he experienced the sadness occasioned by the unfairness of imputed bad motives which called forth his sense of injustice. To a friend he wrote : " With all my Quakerism I cannot but sometimes give way to indignant feeling, when my best motives are tortured into evil ones."

But Whittier was a keen politician; he had a quite unusual insight into human nature, and could handle men dexterously. His judgment was sound, and his knowledge of local conditions exact. " His own county of Essex," one of his fellow countrymen has said, " was then as now noted for the adroitness of its politicians, but at twenty-five J. Greenleaf Whittier could beat the best of them at their own game. The hand of the master is seen in his published letters to Caleb Cushing and to Henry Clay. It was he who devised the coalitions which sent Cushing the Whig, and Rantoul the Democrat, to Congress, which made Boutwell Governor of Massachusetts, and sent Sumner to the United States Senate."

One day in the autumn of 1833, a messenger from Boston arrived at Whittier's farm with an urgent appeal from Garrison, asking him to go to Philadelphia to help a little group of resolute men to form a National Anti-Slavery Society, and to hold its first meeting there. Whittier answered:

I long to go to Philadelphia to urge upon the members of my own Society the duty of putting their shoulders to the work, to make their solemn testimony against slavery visible over the whole land; to urge them by the holy memories of Woolman, Benezet and Tyson to come up, as of old, to the standard of Divine Truth, though even the fires of another persecution should blaze around them. But the expenses of the journey will, I fear, be too much for me, as thou knows our farming business does not put much cash in our pockets. I am, however, greatly obliged to the Boston Young Men's Association for selecting me as one of their delegates.

One of the earliest supporters of the cause of emancipation, Samuel Sewell, removed the financial difficulty, and the journey to Philadelphia was undertaken by stage coach. Whittier was joined by others on the same errand, and far into the night he and Garrison discussed arrangements for the meeting to be held on the following day.

Whittier thus describes the eventful evening:

The Declaration with its few verbal amendments carefully engrossed on parchment, was brought before the convention. Samuel May rose to read it for the last time. His sweet persuasive voice faltered with the intensity of his emotions as he repeated the solemn pledges of the concluding paragraphs. After a season of silence, David Thurston, of Maine, rose, as his name was called by one of the secretaries, and affixed his signature to the document. One after another passed up to the platform, signed, and retired in silence. All felt the deep responsibility of the occasion; the shadow and forecast of a life-long struggle rested upon each countenance.

Of his own signature to this Declaration, Whittier said " I set a higher value on my name as appended to the Anti-Slavery Declaration of 1833, than on the title of any of my books."

Popular feeling became so strong against the Abolitionists that all who sympathized with them were in personal danger. It was a crime to teach a negro to read or to hide a runaway slave, but Whittier encouraged all those who took part in the conflict against slavery, and we have a letter addressed to Dr. Channing on the subject in which he says :

A recent perusal of thy sermons has induced me, although a stranger, to address thee. From all that I have seen of thy writings, it has seemed to me that it was thy aim to make Christianity a practical matter ; a living and beneficent reality such as its Founder intended, a real bond of holy brotherhood which should unite all the human family, unshackle mind and body, and bless all the children of our Heavenly Father with that liberty wherewith He has made them free. To my mind the elevated sentiment in some passages has a direct bearing upon the slavery question. I am but an humble individual, and were my subject less important I should not seek with my feeble voice the ear of one whose name and fame have no narrower limits than those of Christianity itself. May I beg of thee to openly co-operate with that great and deserved influence which Providence has allotted to thy profession with those who are now striving in this cause, to break every chain of selfishness, to enlarge and invigorate the kind affections, to identify themselves with others, to sympathize not with a few but with all the living and rational creatures of God.

Channing responded warmly and threw in his sympathy with the Anti-Slavery cause, so that after his death Whittier wrote of him thus :

> For even in a faithless day
>   Can we our sainted ones discern ;
> And feel, while with them on the way,
>   Our hearts within us burn.
>
> * * * * *
>
> With us was one, who, calm and true,
>   Life's highest purpose understood,
> And, like his blessed Master, knew
>   The joy of doing good.*

One of the greatest difficulties in fighting a long accepted system of iniquity is that half measures of reform are often consented to by the enemy, with the secret purpose of using them to forward his own ends. It was so in this case, and in order to understand the root of opposition manifested against the Abolitionists, we must remember that the colonization scheme was favoured by many philanthropists who thought it a means of gradually extinguishing slavery. It was discovered that the slaveholders used it as a means of ridding them-

* "Channing."

selves of the free coloured people, who made the slaves restless and at times aided them in making their escape. This colonization scheme they advertised as a method of sending Christianity to Africa! Garrison denounced this in no measured terms as the "handmaid" of slavery, and we can well believe that this brought a storm of anger upon him and his friends from the churches. They had even gone so far as to flatter themselves they were doing good mission work, and were taking collections to support it!

This being so, we need not be surprised to read that clergymen, statesmen, and merchants, were greatly angered when their pet philanthropy was denounced as a "bulwark of slavery." Whittier and Garrison stood their ground side by side, maintaining their position, and when George Thompson, M.P., of England, visited the country in 1834, he did much to strengthen their cause. "As an orator he surpassed any speaker I have ever heard," said Garrison; but he was soon accused of making trouble between the North and South for the benefit of the merchants and manufacturers of England. Whittier replied :

Rail on then, brethren of the South,
  Ye shall not hear the truth the less ;
No seal is on the Yankee's mouth,
  No fetter on the Yankee's press !
From our Green Mountains to the sea,
One voice shall thunder—We are free.*

We have in a letter written by Whittier, a description of one of the Boston riots at this time when he was at a session of the legislature, in which he says :

I found the street thronged and noisy with turbulent respectability and unwashed rascality. I was anxious about my young sister, who I knew was in a woman's anti-slavery meeting ; but I heard the ladies had left and were safe. The fury of the mob seemed to be directed against G. Thompson, but failing to find him they seized upon Garrison. I heard their shout of exultation and caught a glimpse of their victim just as he was rescued and driven off to Leverett Street jail. Thither S. May and myself followed, and visited him in prison. I could sympathize with him for only a short time before the Concord mob, which could not get hold of Thompson, fell upon me with stones and missiles, and my escape with nothing worse than bruises was something to be thankful for. The rioters had just roughly used a poor Quaker

* "Stanzas for the Times."

preacher quietly passing through the town who had the misfortune of being mistaken for myself. It seemed to be a case of suffering by proxy all round.

Elizabeth Whittier writes of this visit of G. Thompson :

The shameful record must be written down that in this land of Bibles and law and learning and freedom a minister of Christ—a Paul in his zeal for the promotion of every cause of righteousness and truth—a stranger, led by the holiest impulses of humanity, coming among us to proclaim in his own wonderful and fervid eloquence the eternal principles of justice to mankind—that such a man with such purposes, was slandered by Americans, hated by Americans, and mobbed by Americans ; that in Massachusetts thousands of dollars were offered for his assassination ! Oh, I am sure I shall never be proud of my country.

Elizabeth had thrown herself into the movement with all the eagerness of her enthusiastic nature. She united in forming a Female Anti-Slavery Society, and on hearing the first annual meeting was to be held in Boston, and the Rev. Samuel May was to address the meeting, she decided to go. The appeal on behalf of the two-and-a-half millions of their countrymen was listened to with breathless attention when suddenly there was heard a sound of heavy footsteps and angry voices, and stones came flying through the windows from the crowd below. Before long the Mayor, followed by the police, forced his way through the crowd, and called to the women, "Go home, go home, if you would not see bloodshed. I can protect you now, but not for long."

Elizabeth and her friend, Harriet May, placed themselves on either side of the speaker, each taking one of his hands. They were well known in the city, and on seeing Samuel May under the charge of the two women, a roar of vexation went up from the crowd, and many fell back ashamed and afraid to carry out their purpose. Garrison was seized and dragged through the streets by a rope thrown round him by which they meant to hang him. He was rescued, however, with great difficulty. Again and again Whittier was pelted with rotten eggs, mud, and stones, and said afterwards he could remember the sound of the stones that struck the ground round him, and that he could realize how St.

Paul felt when he was thrice stoned. But more often than not the indignities he received were meant for someone else, the men being frenzied through drink, thus not recognising one from another. In after years Whittier met a man who confessed he was one of the mob. Whittier asked what would have been done with Thompson and himself, and the man told him preparations had been made to blacken their faces so that they could not remove the colour, and tar and feathers were to follow. On another occasion after being assailed with rotten eggs and missiles in company with a minister, Whittier said : " I am surprised that we should be disturbed in a quiet Puritan city like Newburyport, I've lived near it for years and thought it a pious city ! " Laying his hand on his shoulder, the minister said, " Young man, when you are as old as I am, you will understand that it is easier to be pious than it is to be good ! "

With all this Whittier was able to write to his friend Thayer " Anti-Slavery is going on well in spite of mobs, Andover Seminary, and *rum*."

CHAPTER V.

J. GREENLEAF WHITTIER, though barely thirty years of age, was beginning to feel, through repeated failures in health, that he could not continue the oversight of the Haverhill farm in addition to his Anti-Slavery work, writing for the papers, getting up petitions, attending conventions, and an enormous correspondence. His mother and Aunt Mercy were requiring more care, and the distance from the Meeting House was an increasing difficulty. His brother and eldest sister had both married, and there was no longer any need for so large a house.

So in the spring of 1836, the farm of one hundred and forty-eight acres was sold, and the family settled down in a cottage which Whittier bought, in the village of Amesbury, near the Friends' Meeting House. The poet had by this time given up all hope of marriage. He had his mother, aunt, and sister to care for; and though it is very evident that the sacrifice was a real one, Cornelia Russ not having been his only love, he was able to write in his old age, " My life has been on the whole quite as happy as I deserved, or had a right to expect. I know there has been something very sweet and beautiful missed, but I have no reason to complain. I have learned at last to look into happiness with the eyes of others, and to thank God for the happy unions and holy firesides I have known."

On a friend once asking him if he would publish her favourite poem called " Memories," he said, " I love it too; but hardly know whether to publish it, it is so personal and near my heart." And as we read it, we understand.

> How thrills once more the lengthening chain
>   Of memory, at the thought of thee!
> Old hopes which long in dust have lain,
> Old dreams, come thronging back again,
>   And boyhood lives again in me;
> I feel its glow upon my cheek,
>   Its fulness of the heart is mine,
> As when I leaned to hear thee speak,
>   Or raised my doubtful eye to thine.

I hear again thy low replies,
  I feel thy arm within my own,
And timidly again uprise
The fringèd lids of hazel eyes,
  With soft brown tresses overblown.
Ah! memories of sweet summer eves,
  Of moonlit wave and willowy way,
Of stars and flowers, and dewy leaves,
  And smiles and tones more dear than they!

Yet hath thy spirit left on me
  An impress Time has worn not out,
And something of myself in thee,
A shadow from the past, I see,
  Lingering, even yet, thy way about;
Not wholly can the heart unlearn
  That lesson of its better hours,
Not yet has Time's dull footstep worn
  To common dust that path of flowers.

But as we sigh at the thought of what might have been, we know that the poet's home life was filled with unusually tender associations. His younger sister, the beloved Elizabeth, was an increasing joy to him; highly gifted, full of merriment and ready wit, and well able to sympathize in her brother's poetic nature, she responded to his love with warm affection. She was his literary companion, and a charming hostess to his friends, and it was Whittier's opinion that had her health permitted she might have taken a high position as a writer.

A pastor in Newburyport, T. W. Higginson, spoke of her as "one of the rarest of women . . . a woman never to be forgotten, and no one can truly estimate the long celibate life of the poet without bearing in mind that he had for many years at his own fireside the concentrated wit and sympathy of womankind in this sister."

Lucy Larcom, Elizabeth's dearest friend, gives us a picture of the home life that leaves nothing surely to be desired.

If I could not think of them together there, of the quiet light which bathes everything within and around their cottage, under the shadow of the hill, of the care repaid by gentle trust, and the dependence so blessed in its shelter of tenderness and strength, the world would seem to me a much drearier place; for I have never seen anything like this brother's and sister's love and the home atmosphere it creates, the belief in human goodness, and the Divine love it diffuses into all who enter the charmed circle.

The new cottage in which the poet, his mother and sister took up their abode, was pleasantly situated below the hill on which Amesbury lay. The river Merrimac flowed by the side of the meadows, and from the cottage there were fine views of wooded scenery. At the end of the building, which was only one storey high, there was the garden room overlooking the orchard, and this was Greenleaf's study. The northeast window was in a door opening on to a verandah, and this pleasant room was the one generally in use, as Whittier could write undisturbed in the midst of the family concerns. It was here that most of his friends enjoyed intercourse with the poet, and here that "Snow-Bound" and nearly all his best work was done.

Whittier's reputation as a writer and a politician was growing, and men were beginning to have faith in him as a reformer. To his shrewd knowledge of mankind he added much skill in handling the weapons of warfare. He encouraged men to go with him as far as they could, and would accept assistance from apparently unfriendly sources. To a friend who was complaining to him of some party leader, Whittier said, "has thee found many saints or angels in thy dealings with either political party? Do not expect too much of human nature." He himself never worked for any personal advantages, was faithful to his party, but never allowed his politics to weaken his Christianity.

On one occasion he took one of his poorer neighbours to the Town House on election day. The man promised to vote for Whittier if he would give him a lift in his waggon. Whittier thought it best to watch him, and on going to the ballot-box was mortified to see an opposition vote dropped into the box. "Did not take the man home, did you?" asked a friend on hearing the story. "O yes, I did," he said, "I promised his wife I would see him home safely, and I had to do it. I took him home dead drunk in the bottom of my waggon."

For many years at Amesbury, his friends were almost exclusively those who were engaged in fighting the slave trade, men and women of tremendous energy and will who were giving up their lives to the cause, so that Harriet Martineau speaks of that period as "the martyr age of the United States."

THE INTERIOR OF THE KITCHEN AT THE HOMESTEAD.

Letter after letter to the papers and to private friends kept Whittier hard at work; and visits to Boston and New York for weeks at a time, to advance the Anti-Slavery cause, injured his health and again laid him aside. But poems were continually appearing on the slavery question such as "Our Fellow Countrymen in Chains," "The Hunters of Men," "Song of the Free," and many more. Personal appeals were sent to public men, and as one of them in an address besought all classes to abstain from discussing the subject of slavery, Whittier replied :

We can neither permit the gag to be thrust in our mouths by others, on deem it the part of patriotism to place it there ourselves . . . Is this the age, are ours the laws, are the sons of the Pilgrim Fathers the men for advice like this ? Far fitter is it for the banks of the Bosphorus, and the Neva.

In the year 1837, Benjamin Lundy, worn out in the cause to which he had given his life, retired from the editorship of an Anti-Slavery paper and begged Whittier to take up the gauntlet he was laying down.

Whittier responded to the call and became editor of the *Pennsylvania Freeman*. To take up work dropped from such a hand was an inspiration in itself.

Benjamin Lundy, a poor orphan Quaker, when struggling as a youth at his trade of saddler, saw gangs of miserable slaves chained together on their way to the plantations further South, heard the driver's whip, and determined, as the sense of the iniquity entered his soul, that as soon as he could help them he would endeavour to right their wrongs.

He started a newspaper, had to walk twenty miles every week to the printer's to fetch the papers, and then tramp the country to sell them. He walked in the depth of winter 125 miles to enlist Garrison's help in editing his newspaper. Thus he toiled on, year in, year out, till an old man, bent with age and worn out in the cause, he sought for one to champion his paper, and Whittier pledged himself to continue it and fight for Freedom with undiminished zeal.

The Anti-Slavery Society by this time was so far gaining the confidence of many leading Americans, that a large hall called Pennsylvania Hall was being erected at a cost of $43,000 that the work for liberty, and equality of civil rights, might be advanced and the evil of slavery be abolished. The large hall was to accommodate two thousand persons, and a newspaper office for Whittier was attached to the building.

As soon as all was in order it was arranged to hold a convention lasting three days to commemorate the opening of the hall.

Everthing passed off satisfactorily on the first day. On the next morning a meeting of the Female Anti-Slavery Society was to be held. At an early hour the building was packed, but soon after the preliminary details were over shouts and hisses were heard from the outside, and then stones followed and danger seemed imminent.

The dignity and calmness of the women, however, made a deep impression. One, who was on the platform, rose and said in a clear voice :

It is not the crashing of these windows, nor the maddening rush of those voices that calls me before you. But it is the still small voice within which may not be withstood that bids me open my mouth for the dumb, that bids me plead the cause of God's perishing ones.

This Quaker lady, Angelina Grimké, a most devoted worker in the cause she had espoused, spoke for more than an hour on the sin of slavery. She was listened to attentively, and when the meeting broke up the speakers and hearers were allowed to pass out unhurt. It is doubtful if many on the day of their marriage would have done as Angelina Grimké did, for an added interest to the excitement of that occasion is attached to the fact that in the evening Miss Grimké was married to Mr. Weld, and Whittier that night wrote a congratulatory poem for the occasion.

On the following morning, determined hostility once more gained the mastery. Placards were pasted on the city walls encouraging rioters to do their worst. The Mayor refused to take any steps to protect the abolitionists, and in the evening some 15,000 people were in the streets. It was thought better to suspend the meeting, but the rioters rushed to the doors, forced them open, turned on the gas, piled up every thing they could lay their hands on that would burn, and then set fire to the building. The fire engines were called out, but on arriving at the scene of action, the mob drove them off and prevented a drop of water from being thrown on to the flames.

Whittier endeavoured to expostulate by addressing the crowd, but had to fly for his life. He went to the house of a friend, Dr. Parish, donned a wig and long white overcoat, and returned to the crowd, making his way to his office to secure some papers he wished to save from destruction. He was not recognised, and, as one of the crowd, did as he liked. His paper, *The Freeman*, went to press on the following day with this notice of the outrage :

18th of Fifth Month, half past seven o'clock.— Pennsylvania Hall is in ashes ! The beautiful temple consecrated to liberty has been offered a smoking sacrifice to the Demon of Slavery. In the heart of this city a flame has gone up to heaven. It will be seen from Maine to Georgia. In its red and lurid light men will see more clearly than ever the black abominations of the fiend at whose instigation it was kindled. We have no time for comment. Let the abhorred deed speak for itself. Let all men see by what a frail tenure they hold property and life in a land overshadowed by the curse of slavery.

On the following day a meeting was held in front of the smoking ruins. No interruption was made while Whittier spoke and sustained a resolution that the right of suffrage should be held sacred to the cause of freedom.

Continued anxiety prevailed. A new building for sheltering coloured orphans was burned down, a church belonging to the coloured people was attacked, and also an office that advocated free discussions.

To J. E. Fuller, Whittier writes :—

They leave no stone unturned to put us down. The clergy of all denominations are preaching against us. The politicians are abusing us in their papers, and dirty penny sheets, with most outrageous caricatures of Garrison, Thompson, Angelina Grimké Weld, are hawked about the streets. But we shall go ahead nevertheless. The abolitionists of Old Pennsylvania are of the right material. I admire and honor their stern moral courage in manfully maintaining their ground against a fiendish and bitter opposition.*

Whittier felt that a volume of his Anti-Slavery Poems might be of use just then, and he authorized Joseph Healy at the head of the Society to publish them. It comprised fifty poems and selections from his miscellaneous works.

* Pickard, 239.

On the title-page he quotes those renowned words of S. T. Coleridge:—

"There is a time to keep silence," saith Solomon. But when I proceeded to the first verse of the fourth chapter of the Ecclesiastes, "and considered all the oppressions that are done under the sun; beheld the tears of such as are oppressed, and they have had no comforter; and on the side of the oppressors there was power," I concluded this was not the time to keep silence; for Truth should be spoken at all times, but more especially at those times when to speak Truth is dangerous.

The excitement connected with the riots, the strain of editorial work and his "ringing words of encouragement" in every direction, made it necessary for Whittier to seek some respite from his labours. He took a tour in Western Pennsylvania, but could not help working wherever he went. Then a visit to the Saratoga Springs followed, where he was much enlivened, not by drinking the water but by the amusement he gained in studying human nature. A visit to Newport with his cousins brought his wanderings to an end. He was much refreshed, and immediately on his return he was deputed to go through Pennsylvania and employ seventy speakers, if he could find them, to awaken the national conscience on the subject of Freedom.

In January of the following year he visited Washington, and was in the gallery of the House of Representatives during the great debate on the right of petition which ended in the shutting out of all petitions upon the subject of slavery.*

"Northern subserviency has yielded *all* to the demands of the South," so he said.

Again his friends became anxious about his health. The physician discovered serious heart trouble, and insisted on his giving up the editorship of *The Freeman*. Increasing pain and weakness showed him he must submit, and reluctantly he wrote his "Farewell" to the paper, and he and Elizabeth returned to Amesbury for the winter.

---

* Pickard, 253.

CHAPTER VI.

FOR a time Whittier settled down with his family at Amesbury, and everything was done that their slender means would allow to further his complete recovery.

He never, however, regained any measure of what could be called good health, and his own poverty which prevented him from doing what he would have liked to do for his mother and sister weighed on his mind.

His poems were being circulated all over the States, but, through his being so strong an abolitionist, they were not sufficiently remunerative to be a source of reliable income.

A most unexpected help came to him, however, when he was in considerable anxiety about ways and means.

Joseph Sturge, the Quaker philanthropist from England, visited the United States with a memorial from the British Friends on the subject of Slavery. He had worked nobly in his own country for the same cause to which Whittier had devoted his life, and his sympathetic nature was greatly touched when visiting the poet in his home to find it so destitute of the comforts of life, which were necessary for a man in his poor state of health. Before leaving the States, he placed in the hands of a trusted Friend a large sum of money for Whittier to use, as he felt to be desirable.

The poet was deeply touched and thankful for so generous a thought and action, but there are strong suspicions that not a little of the amount found its way to the Anti-Slavery cause.

A very beautiful tribute to Joseph Sturge's memory,* written by Whittier, speaks of him thus :

> His faith and works, like streams that intermingle,
>   In the same channel ran :
> The crystal clearness of an eye kept single
>   Shamed all the frauds of man.
>
> The very gentlest of all human natures
>   He joined to courage strong,
> And love outreaching unto all God's creatures
>   With sturdy hate of wrong.

* "In Remembrance of Joseph Sturge."

> Tender as woman, manliness and meekness
>   In him were so allied
> That they who judged him by his strength
>   or weakness
>   Saw but a single side.
>
> Men failed, betrayed him, but his zeal seemed
>   nourished
>   By failure and by fall;
> Still a large faith in human-kind he cherished,
>   And in God's love for all.

The long period of weakness which followed tried the poet when he wanted to be up and doing, and we feel the struggle as he writes:

> Oh power to do! Oh baffled will!
>   Oh prayer and action! ye are one.
> Who may not strive, may yet fulfil
>   The harder task of standing still,
> And good but wished with God is done!*

No doubt the physical weakness produced depression which was hardly a natural characteristic, but we find him at this time lamenting to a friend over "seasons of doubt and darkness," and saying

My temperament, ardent, impetuous, imaginative, powerfully acted upon from without,

* "The Waiting."

keenly susceptible to all influences from the intellectual world, as well as to those of Nature in her varied manifestations, is, I fear, ill-adapted to that quiet, submissive, introverted state of patient and passive waiting for direction and support under these trials and difficulties.

During this time of weakness he received the sad news of the sudden death of Lucy Hooper.

Whittier had made her acquaintance when in New York, and was a frequent visitor at the Hoopers' house. Lucy was then quite young and very charming, and her poetical talent drew them together. Many of her poems appeared in the *Pennsylvania Freeman*, and Whittier urged her to write one of considerable length which he believed would be received with much enthusiasm. A memorable walk by the banks of Merrimac is recalled in his poem " Lucy Hooper," in which he speaks of her beaiutful character:

> The memory of thy loveliness
>   Shall round our weary pathway smile,
> Like moonlight when the sun has set,
> A sweet and tender radiance yet.

Thoughts of thy clear-eyed sense of duty,
  Thy generous scorn of all things wrong,
The truth, the strength, the graceful beauty
  Which blended in thy song.
All lovely things, by thee beloved,
  Shall whisper to our hearts of thee;
These green hills, where thy childhood roved,
  Yon river winding to the sea,
The sunset light of autumn eves
  Reflecting on the deep, still floods,
Cloud, crimson sky, and trembling leaves
  Of rainbow-tinted woods,
These, in our view, shall henceforth take
A tenderer meaning for thy sake.

To her sisters he writes :

I was not prepared for such a termination of her illness. Sick myself, I cannot write you a long letter, nor perhaps would you wish it. What can I say to comfort you. What condolence can I offer to those who have been able fully to understand and appreciate the purity and beauty of the spirit which has just passed from among you ? He alone, who loveth those whom He chasteneth, can comfort and sustain you under such a trial as yours. To Him, who hath taken to the arms of His love our dear Lucy, I can alone commend you. Do write me, and let me know the many particulars of her last illness, and the last mournful scene. I am no stranger with a stranger's careless curiosity. I have had few friends so dear to me—so often in my thoughts—as Lucy. She is not gone. Her pure affections, her fine intellect, her faith and love and simple trust in her Heavenly Father are not lost.

Whittier's friends were more to him, it has been thought, than to most men, and though he kept up a correspondence with many leading men of his time, his familiar acquaintances were chiefly women. With them he was free, at his ease, ready to give and take and humbly to acknowledge superiority when he saw it, as in the case of Lucy Hooper.

His cousin, Ann Wendell, was one with whom he had much religious sympathy, and his correspondence with her on spiritual matters is deeply interesting. In some of his letters we see how he was moved at the language of encouragement offered him more than once by friends who felt he had been called to high service for the cause of humainty. But he is ever conscious of his own shortcomings. "The longer I live," he says to his cousin, " I see the evil in myself in a clearer light and more that is good in others and if I do not grow better I am constrained to be more charitable."

In one letter addressed to Ann Wendell, he expresses his keen interest in what was taking place in the religious world in England.

8mo., 1843.

I should be heartily glad to visit Philadelphia, to sit with cousin Ann, and discuss upon the great problems of human life and destiny, and not upon those high abstractions alone, but upon the household things, the simple, the tender and the beautiful of daily life, which " Lie scattered at the feet of man like flowers," and talk with thy mother about Luther, Melancthon, and Pope and Cardinal, and Fathers and Councils. Speaking of these matters, does thee read much of the Puseyism controversy which is now going on? The English Episcopal Church seems ready to go over to Popery in earnest. Has thee noticed the general tendency towards the old trust in man —in priests, sacrifices, and ghostly mummery and machinery? . . . I have a strong faith; it seems almost like prophecy, that the result will be, ere the lapse of two centuries, a complete and permanent change in the entire Christian world. Weary and disgusted with shams and shadows, with the effort to believe a few miserable worms of the dust the sole dispensers of Heaven's salvation, men will awake to the simple beauty of practical Christianity . . . To me, Quaker and Catholic are alike, both children of my Heavenly Father, and separated only by a *creed*, to some, indeed, a barrier like a Chinese wall, but to me frail and slight as a spider's web."

In March, 1844, James Russell Lowell was pressing Whittier " to cry aloud and spare not against the cursed Texas plot." He himself had written some lines against the annexation of Texas, beginning :—

> Rise up, New England, buckle on your mail
>   of proof sublime ;
> Your stern old hate of tyranny, your deep
>   contempt of crime ;
> A plot is hatching now, more full of woe and
>   shame
> Than ever from the iron heart of bloodiest
>   despot came.*

It was published anonymously and was generally thought to be Whittier's till he responded by sending a poem, " Texas : Voice of New England," which was published in the following month. It was thought a little fierce, but the editor, Buckingham, said " Something must be pardoned to the spirit of liberty."

* "Texas."

Both Lowell's and Whittier's poems, however, did much to arouse a deep feeling of antagonism to slavery.

Ill health kept Whittier at home, but he was not idle. Poem after poem appeared; "Ichabod," "Maud Muller," "To my Old Schoolmaster," "A Sabbath Scene," "Mary Garvin," "The Angel of Patience" and "Tauler" being some of those best known.

Though he was little over forty years of age, he felt at times as if his work was nearly done.

"I feel a growing disinclination," he writes, "to pen and ink—overworked, tired by the long weary years of the Anti-Slavery struggle—I want mental rest. I have already lived a long life, if thought and action constitute it."

These waves of depression, however, were followed by times of refreshment, and on sending Sumner a poem entitled "The Wish of To-day," for *The Era*, he received such a gracious reply as set his heart singing again. "Your poem," said Sumner, "has touched my heart. May God preserve you in strength and courage for all your good works. There are few to whom I would allot a larger measure of the world's blessings than to yourself, had I any control, for there are few who deserve them more."

"What Providence has in store for me I know not," wrote Whittier, "but my heart is full of thankfulness that I have been permitted to do something for the cause of humanity, and that with all my sins and errors I have not been suffered to live wholly for myself."

Though often down-hearted at the slowness with which humanity could be roused to a great realisation of injustice, and the unworthy difficulties placed in the way of reform, he never lost hope that the end which the abolitionists had in view would be achieved.

> We bore, as Freedom's hope forlorn,
> The private hate, the public scorn;
> Yet held through all the paths we trod
> Our faith in man and trust in God.
>
> We prayed and hoped; but still with awe,
> The coming of the sword we saw;
> We heard the nearing steps of doom,
> We saw the shade of things to come.

In his poem "Pæan" he shows us that he began to see the efforts put forth were bearing fruit, that the North was thoroughly roused, that the dawn of day was not so far distant, "the dreary night was well nigh passed" and they might take courage.

Another unseen power was at work which was to sweep the country, and thrill the hearts of men and women from North to South, from East to West, through the hand of a woman.

Mrs. Beecher Stowe was writing "Uncle Tom's Cabin" and it was to be issued in serial form. The story soon began to excite intense interest, and sold in increasing numbers as it drew to a close, so that 300,000 copies were bought up during its first year in book form.

The vivid portrayal of the wrongs and horrors of slavery stirred the people of the North profoundly, and the book found its way to the South, where it raised intense excitement and the wildest anger. Publications were hurried through the press to bring discredit upon Mrs. Stowe and her story. They followed one another in the most vehement manner in order to lessen the impression which had been made. But all in vain, and though Mrs. Stowe had related as of ordinary occurrence incidents that were in a measure exceptional, the iniquity of slavery was brought home to thousands of hearts never before stirred at the wickedness of the system, and the impression made has never been obliterated.

In the early Spring of 1848, John Quincy Adams passed away. Whittier was much moved by the event. He had visited Washington a few days previously, and had had an interview with Adams, of which he wrote to Charles Sumner :

Ere this thou hast doubtless heard of the sudden illness of the venerable Adams. His death will be the fitting end of such a glorious life. Falling at his post, dying with his harness on, in the capitol so often shaken by his noble battle for freedom ! My eyes fill with tears, but the emotion is not unmingled with a feeling of joy that such a man should thus pass from us. A few days ago I had a highly interesting conversation with him. All his old vigour seemed to re-animate him when he touched on the subject of slavery. I shall never forget that interview. On that gray discrowned head the entire fury of slave-holding arrogance and wrath was expended.

CHAPTER VII

IT may be well to pause for a moment in the story of Whittier's life that we may consider his religious position, and the spring from which his thoughts welled up into word and action.

It is difficult for the present generation to realize the profound change which has taken place in the theological world since the middle of the last century.

The heathen notion of a Deity who must be appeased had crept into the Christian conception of God at a very early period. The fact of His fatherhood, so dear to Christ, was rarely, if ever, referred to. A terror surrounded the very thought of God to little children, and they turned from Him to Jesus Christ as one far more tender and compassionate.

Then it began to dawn upon the Christian communities that the teaching of Jesus Christ was altogether different from that which they had been taught to believe, and that His real mission was to *reveal* the *love* of God to men. The Society of Friends, never given to theological subtleties, had always exalted and emphasised the love of God, and the spirit of God in men's own hearts which could respond to that love.

Whittier was born into the Society of Friends. His ancestors for generations had been Quakers, and he inherited by birth and training those principles upon which the Society has been built and which have developed some of the truest saints in England and America.

The Puritans laid great stress on the external aspect of religion: their conception of redemption emphasised the outward transaction; and their salvation was an escape from Hell; all objectively existing outside of the individual. Fox taught that redemption was a process wrought within, and that salvation was being saved from sin, not merely from its consequences, an experience that led the Friends to testify by their *lives* that they were Christians rather than by the acceptance of any creed or dogma.

They believe that God speaks to His people to-day as of old, and that salvation was not made to depend upon the acceptance of any doctrine, but on yielding to the guidance of God's spirit, on "obedience, on self-surrender, and an opening of the soul to the Light."

The early Friends founded their appeal on the fact, as asserted by Jesus Christ, that "the Kingdom of Heaven is within you," the "light that lighteth every man that cometh into the world." From this all the distinctive tenets of the Friends follow.

Whittier says, "I am thankful to the Divine providence which placed me where I am with an unshaken faith in the Light within—the immanence of the Divine Spirit in Christianity, 'Where the spirit of the Lord is there is Liberty.'"

And in looking forward, he emphasises the fact of the Inward Light:

> They fail to read clearly the sign of the times who do not see that the hour is coming when under the searching eye of the philosopher, and the terrible analysis of science, the letter and the outward evidence will not altogether avail us, when the surest dependence must be upon the light of Christ confirming the truth of outward Scripture by inward experience, for it has its witness in all human hearts.

His words were prophetic, and in reading them we turn to the present day philosopher Eucken, one of the greatest thinkers of our time, who expresses his convictions thus :

The individual awakening is in becoming conscious of the absolute spiritual life and identifying himself with it. We not only see Light in His light ; we kindle our light at His.*

Christianity does not bring to man mere teaching and theories, not merely a world-wide view but a great realm of fact standing above all argument, caprice or mood.

Again he says:

We must insist more strongly than ever that the salvation which religion promises to man is a salvation not of his natural but of his spiritual self, that it imposes on him a momentous choice, and demands of him heavy sacrifices.†

This statement is in full harmony with Whittier's position when he says :

The future hope of our religion lies not in setting the letter above the spirit, not in substituting type and symbol and oriental figure

* *Eucken and Bergson.* By Mrs. Hermann, 28, 98, 102.
† Quoted by R. M. Jones, *American Friend*, XIV., 803.

and hyperbole for the simple truths they were meant to represent; not in the schools of theology, not in much speaking and noise and vehemence, but in heeding more closely the inward guide and teacher.

Whittier never confused theology and religion, one a science, the other a life:

"I regard Christianity," he says, "as a life rather than a creed. My ground of hope for myself and for humanity is in that Divine fulness of love which was manifested in the life, teachings, and self-sacrifice of Christ."

He was conscious that love revealed God to us, and our knowledge of Him must be in proportion to the extent of our love, for "Everyone that *loveth* is begotten of God and *knoweth* God."

He did not, however, undervalue a sound belief. "The truth should be held, but at the same time I believe it may be held in unrighteousness."

His attitude towards Jesus Christ is thus indicated: "In Him we see the essential character of God." He is the ultimate standard by which we must test all lives, "and humanity can never reach its best apart from Christ."

"Of one thing," he says, "I am certain. I feel that something outside of myself speaks to me and holds me to duty, warns, approves and reproves. It is good, for it requires me to be good, it is wise for it knows the thoughts and intents of the heart. It is to me a revelation of God, and of His character and attributes; the one important fact before which all others seem insignificant."

Thus we feel he held the balance true: the objective Christ, and the subjective Christ; the inner Light responding to the outer.

No poet knew his Bible better or was more influenced by it than Whittier; but he knew at the same time that "the letter killeth, the spirit giveth life," and though he wrote,

> And weary seekers at the best,
> We come back ladened from our quest,
> To find that all the sages said
> Is in the Book our mothers read,

his Christianity was not of the letter, but of the spirit, and his life-long endeavour was to be obedient to that spirit, leading him, through humiliation and failure, "over rough roads and against opposing forces—always *uphill*."

> He set his face against the blast
>   His feet against the flinty shard,
> Till the hard service grew, at last,
>   Its own exceeding great reward.*

He realized the need of pain and sorrow in the training of the soul, he knew without this discipline life might be more pleasant but not so divine.

His distinction between the sinner and the saint is characteristic and sound :

It is the conquering of innate selfish propensities that makes the saint ; and the giving up unduly to impulses that in their origin are necessary to the preservation of life that makes the sinner.

In regard to his tolerance and wide charity nothing can state the position he held better than a quotation from an article of his in the *Friends' Review*, published in 1870 :

A very large proportion of my dearest personal friends are outside of our communion ; and I have learned with John Woolman to find no " narrowness respecting sects and opinions." I cheerfully recognise and bear testimony to the good works and lives of those who widely differ in faith and practice ; but I have seen no

* "Sumner."

truer types of Christianity, no better men and women than I have known, and still know, among those who, not blindly, but intelligently, hold the doctrines and maintain the testimonies of our early Friends.

I bear a willing testimony to the zeal and devotion of some dear friends, who, lamenting the low condition and worldliness too apparent among us, seek to awaken a stronger spiritual life by the partial adoption of the practices, forms and creeds of more demonstrative sects. The great apparent activity of these sects seems to them to contrast very strongly with our quietness and reticence; and they do not always pause to inquire whether the result of this activity is a truer life of practical Christianity than is found in our select gatherings.

His views in relation to the eternal future show a keen insight, we venture to think, into the love of God and the teaching of Jesus Christ. He states his convictions very clearly as follows:

I am not a universalist, for I believe in the possibility of the perpetual loss of a soul that persistently turns away from God in the next life as in this. But I do believe that the Divine love and compassion follow us in all worlds, and the Heavenly Father will do the best that is possible for every creature that He has made.

What that will be must be left to His infinite wisdom and goodness.

All is of God that is, and is to be,
And God is good. Let that suffice for me.

In his poem " The Answer " we see the striking way in which he expresses his thoughts on this matter :

Though God be good and free be heaven,
   No force divine can love compel ;
And, though the song of sins forgiven
   May sound through lowest hell,

The sweet persuasion of His voice
   Respects thy sanctity of will.
He giveth day : thou hath thy choice
   To walk in darkness still.

No word of doom may shut thee out,
   No wind of wrath may downward whirl,
No swords of fire keep watch about
   The open gates of pearl.

Forever round the Mercy-seat
   The guiding lights of Love shall burn ;
But what if, habit-bound, thy feet
   Shall lack the will to turn ?

Oh, doom beyond the saddest guess,
   As the long years of God unroll,
To make thy dreary selfishness
   The prison of thy soul!

> To doubt the love that fain would break
> The fetters from thy self-bound limb;
> And dream that God can thee forsake
> As thou forsakest Him!

But while he held these views he endeavoured, as he wrote to Dr. Farrar, to do something to persuade men of the lesson that " God is a loving Father and not a terrible Moloch."

His old friend, Joshua Coffin, who had been so kind to him in his boyhood, held the terrible doctrine of Predestination as taught at that time, and one day Whittier said to him, " Joshua, don't thee hate God who has doomed thee to everlasting torment ? " " Why, no, it is for the good of all that some are punished." " Joshua, thee has spent thy life doing good, and now thee is of course getting ready to do all the hurt thee can to thy fellow men ! " " No, indeed, my feelings have not changed in the least in this regard." " Thee is going to hell then in this mood ? " " Why, yes, I am reconciled to the will of God, and have no ill feelings towards Him or my race." " Now Joshua, thee is going to hell with a heart full of love for everybody, what can the devil find for such a one as thee to do?" The good man laughed at the idea of the puzzle Satan would be in to find occupation for him, and his depression passed away.

When Joshua Coffin died, Whittier wrote the following inscription for his tombstone:

Teacher and Christian rest!
  Thy threescore years and ten,
  Thy work of tongue and pen,
May well abide the test,
  Of love to God and men!
Here let thy pupils pause, and let the slave
Smooth with free hands thy grave!

The future life was very real and sweet to Whittier and he loved to dwell on it. After reading Mrs. Oliphant's "Little Pilgrim" he wrote to a friend: "I like the Little Pilgrim story better than Dante's picture of heaven—an old man sitting eternally on a high chair, and concentric circles of saints, martyrs, and ordinary church members, whirling around him in perpetual gyration, and singing 'Glory.' All I ask is to be free from sin, and to meet the dear ones again."

And so he was able with extreme tenderness and beautiful hope to console and cheer those who were bereaved. Many are still learning the true spirit in which to face their loss by his "Angel of Patience"; and on the death of Joseph Sturge's sister, he wrote:

> Not upon thee or thine the solemn angel
>   Hath evil wrought;
> Her funeral anthem is a glad evangel,—
>   The good die not!
>
> God calls our loved ones, but we lose not wholly
>   What He hath given;
> They live on earth, in thought and deed, as truly
>   As in His heaven.
>
> And she is with thee; in thy path of trial
>   She walketh yet;
> Still with the baptism of thy self-denial
>   Her locks are wet.
>
> Up, then, my brother! Lo, the fields of harvest
>   Lie white in view!
> She lives and loves thee, and the God thou servest
>   To both is true.*

There is little doubt that both in America and in our own country, Whittier's hymns have contributed largely to clearer light

* "To my Friend on the Death of his Sister."

regarding the future, and many perplexed souls have through them been led into peace and joy in God.

John Chadwick, in speaking of the religious influence of Bryant, Emerson, Longfellow, Lowell, Holmes, and Whittier, says the influence of Whittier upon the religious world was greater than that of any of the others. Indeed it has been said, "I would rather give a man or a woman on the verge of a great moral lapse a marked copy of Whittier than any other book in our language."

All his writings and his life were used to right human wrongs and to uplift his fallen brothers and sisters.

A beautiful illustration of this is given in a letter he received one morning. After lingering over it for a long time, he handed it to a friend with whom he was staying, saying, "I wish thee would read that letter," and then with downcast eyes he was silent till it was finished. It was a most pathetic outpouring of the deepest human longing for sympathy, for companionship and uplifting. The lonely woman wrote, she said, to tell Mr. Whittier what his poems had been to her during all the years of her desolate heart-yearning for education, for enlightenment, and for touch with the great outside world. She added:

> In my darkest moments I have found light and comfort in your poems, which I always keep by my side, and as I never expect to have the privilege of looking into your face, I feel that I must tell you, before I leave this world, what you have been through your writings to one, and I have no doubt to many a longing heart and homesick soul. I have never been in a place so dark and hopeless that I could not find light and comfort and hope in your poems, and when I go into my small room and close the door upon the worries and perplexing cares that continually beset me, and sit down by my window that looks out over the hills which have been my only companions, I never fail to find in the volume which is always by my side, some word of peace to my longing heart.

Returning the letter his friend said, "I would rather have the testimony you are constantly receiving from forlorn and hungry souls—the assurance that you are helping God's neglected children—than the crown of any queen on earth."

With tearful eyes he replied, " Such letters greatly humiliate me. I can sometimes write from a high plane, but thee knows I cannot live up to it all the time. I wish I could think I deserved the kind things said of me."

But, though he humbly fancied he was not worthy of such kind thoughts, it was because he so nearly succeeded in living up "on a high plane" that his words carried the influence they exerted. They came from his heart, they were the unconscious echo of his life. "Whence came the power?" says one, and answers, "It is to be found, I believe, in the moral and spiritual elevation of his nature."*

After Charles Kingsley's last interview with Whittier he said, as he left him, "He is a rare old saint."

Illustrations, not a few, could be given of Divine help stealing into sad and broken hearts on reading some of his poems, and a new life springing up from the inspiration that

> Deep below, as high above
> Sweeps the circle of God's love.

A young girl at college, over-strung with work and the difficulties of her life, went to the president and said, "It is of no use, I

* W. Garrett Horder.

cannot go on, my life is a failure, I must leave college and go home."

The president listened, he then reached out his hands and from his book-shelves took down a copy of Whittier's poems. He handed it to his pupil, saying, "Go, and read 'The Grave by the Lake,' and then come back to me and I will talk with you."

After some time the girl returned. "I will overcome the obstacles," she said, "I will go on with my college course. I believe after reading those verses that life *is* worth the effort."

One more story to the same effect must suffice. In a New York prison a poor fallen woman was confined, utterly callous to every effort that had been made to reach her better self. After an unusually violent outbreak of temper, the superintendent took her a copy of Whittier's poems. He asked her if she would read "The Eternal Goodness," and then left her. On returning after some time he found the poor creature still reading, her eyes showing she had been crying. "That is beautiful reading," she said softly, "but is it true what it says? Does God love me?"

The words rested with her and we can understand how she would say over to herself

> And thou O Lord! by whom are seen
> Thy creatures as they be,
> Forgive me if too close I lean
> My human heart on Thee!

From that time a new life began with her.

The Friends' teaching of the Inner Light naturally leads to a realization of the equality of all men in the sight of God, a unity of spirit, and a demand for the freedom of all. From this had developed the philanthropy which is a distinguishing product of Quakerism.

Anti-Slavery, Peace, Temperance work, and religious reform of many kinds for the uplift of mankind, have not ceased since the days of George Fox, and every member of the Society of Friends is expected to take some share in these efforts. We have seen how Whittier, as a young man full of political ambition, was stirred to lay all aside that he might fight the "barbarism of slavery . . . in all its deformity." "I like practical Christianity," he said, "the true following of the Master. I am weary of creeds and dogmas." And he entered into the purpose of the Master who came to "proclaim release to the captives and to set at liberty them that are bruised."

The conception of a Christian life was not with Whittier, as with some poets, the creation of beautiful thoughts with no corresponding life to illustrate them in action. His life was the embodiment of his idyls, and here was the secret of his influence.

Could any words express more concisely, and with more perfect balance, his conception of the teaching of "Our Master" than the following verses?

> Our Friend, our Brother, and our Lord,
>   What may Thy service be?
> Nor name, nor form, nor ritual word,
>   But simply following Thee.
>
> Thy litanies, sweet offices
>   Of love and gratitude;
> Thy sacramental liturgies,
>   The joy of doing good.
>
> To do Thy will is more than praise,
>   As words are less than deeds,
> And simple trust can find Thy ways
>   We miss with chart of creeds.

We faintly hear, we dimly see,
  In differing phrase we pray;
But, dim or clear, we own in Thee
  The Light, the Truth, the Way!

Alone, O love ineffable!
  Thy saving name is given;
To turn aside from Thee is hell,
  To walk with Thee is heaven!

The letter fails, and systems fall,
  And every symbol wanes;
The Spirit over-brooding all,
  Eternal Love remains.*

---

* From "Our Master."

CHAPTER VIII

THOUGH Whittier had contributed his poems to a great number of periodicals there had been no volume published of his works before 1849. Mr. Mussey, a Boston publisher, thought the time had come for him to be acknowledged a poet of considerable merit and that the public would accept him as such. He was prepared to undertake the venture, offering the author five hundred dollars for the copyright, and a royalty on the sales. The book appeared in attractive style, with good engravings, and very soon ran through three editions.

The natural want of confidence in one's self when casting one's thoughts broadcast on the world appears again and again in Whittier, and his literary ventures were submitted to his publishers with a sort of child-like humility. To one he wrote:

However, as they say in the east, Who is my mother's son, that I should presume to dictate to thy superior wisdom? Do as seemeth best in thine own eyes, and I shall take it for granted it *is* best. I have had no leisure when in tolerable health for any polishing of my rhymes. I suppose under any circumstances I ought not to have made any, but *I could not help it.*

In response, however, to a word of praise, he says, " It is only when they are blamed or praised that we fully realize how much we love these bantlings of ours."

The political horizon was full of electricity. No one could tell what storm might come. The "Free Soilers" were to name the United States Senator. Whittier insisted on Sumner being called to take the place of Daniel Webster who had resigned. After some pressure, Sumner consented to stand. Some of the Democrats refused to vote for him. Both he and Whittier felt he had better resign, but the party urged him to remain, which he did.

On April the 24th, 1851, Sumner by a majority of one was elected United States Senator. We see what this meant to Whittier :

I take the earliest moment of ability, after a sudden and severe attack of illness, to congratulate thee, not so much on thy election, as upon the proof which it offers of the turning of the tide—the recoil of the popular feeling—the near and certain doom of the wicked Slave Law. My heart is full of gratitude to God. For when I consider the circumstances of this election, I am constrained to regard it as His work. And I rejoice that thy position is so distinct and emphatic; that thy triumph is such a direct rebuke to politicians, hoary with years of political chicanery and fraud; that unpledged, free, and without a single concession or compromise, thou art enabled to take thy place in the United States Senate. May the good Providence which has overruled the purposes of thy life in this matter, give thee strength and grace to do great things for humanity. I never knew such a general feeling of real heart-pleasure and satisfaction as is manifested by all except inveterate Hunkers, in view of thy election. The whole country is electrified by it. Sick abed, I hear the guns—Quaker as I am—with real satisfaction.

Sumner was nine months in the Senate before he could get any opportunity of making a speech on the great subject for which he consented to stand. Whittier expresses his sympathy with him:

I am by no means surprised at the refusal of the Senate to hear thee. It is simply carrying out the resolutions of the two Baltimore conventions. Never mind. The right time will come for thee, if not this session, the next certainly. I think our proper place for speaking now is to the people directly rather than to Congress. I want thee to put on thy harness this fall and do battle as in '48.

In reply Sumner wrote:

I am grateful for your words of cheer and confidence. I have never desired to come here, as you well know. Since I have been here, our cause has never been out of my mind. In the exercise of my best discretion I have postponed speaking until now. Should I not succeed before the close of the session, I shall feel sad; but I cannot feel that I have failed in a duty. *But I shall speak* on an amendment of the Civil Appropriation Bill. Thus far, whenever I have spoken I have been listened to. On this occasion I may not have the attention; but the speech shall be made. For a long time I have been prepared to handle the Fugitive Slave Bill at length. By the blessing of God it shall be done. . . . I shrink from the political labours to which you beckon me. I have been in my seat every day this session. I long for repose and an opportunity for quiet labours. But more than all things I long to declare myself against the Fugitive Slave Bill. At this moment I can say nothing. My ship is in a terrible calm, like that of the Ancient Mariner. But it will move yet. . . . I notice the withdrawal of confidence from me. Well a-day! I never courted it. I will be content without it. But I shall claim yours.

An event occurred, when Sumner was speaking in the Senate chamber, which stirred Whittier to the very depths of his nature. Preston Brooks of South Carolina struck Sumner down for some words he uttered, and for a moment it was thought he would be deprived of his life.* Fortunately it was not fatal, and Whittier immediately wrote to him:

I have been longing to write to thee, or rather to see thee. God knows my heart has been with thee through thy season of trial and suffering; and now it is full of gratitude and joy that thy life has been spared to us and to freedom.

I have read and re-read thy speech, and I look upon it as thy best. . . It is enough for immortality. So far as thy own reputation is concerned, nothing more is needed. But

---

* From "Historian's History of the World," Vol. xxiii., 397, "P. Brooks from South Carolina approached Sumner, after his speech denouncing a Bill in sympathy with slavery, and rained blow upon blow upon his head till he sank bleeding and unconscious on the floor."

this is of small importance. We cannot see as yet the entire results of that speech, but everything now indicates that it has saved the country. If at the coming election a Free State President is secured, it will be solely through the influence of that speech and the mad fury which its unanswerable logic and fearless exposure of official criminals provoked. Thank God, then, dear Sumner, even in thy sufferings, that He has made the wrath of man to praise Him, and that the remainder of wrath He will restrain. My heart is full and I have much to say ; but I will not weary thee with words.

Ever on the alert, the leaders of the Anti-Slavery movement suggested that a magazine should be started to try to win the sympathy of the lawyers, merchants, and clergy, the classes still perfectly indifferent to the subject, or actively hostile. To ensure success Lowell was engaged as editor, and the *Atlantic Monthly*, as it was called, comprised such writers as Emerson, Whittier, Theodore Parker, Mrs. Stowe, Longfellow, Motley, Prescott, Whipple and Trowbridge.

With such a galaxy of talent success was assured, and in 1857 a new era in

American literature was inaugurated. Most of the leading magazines were not in sympathy with the Liberty party, but here were men who could hold their own and were determined to speak out on a subject that was not popular.

The first number was excellent, the sale was good, and the magazine went steadily on its way. "Emerson is outdoing himself," wrote Whittier, "and the Autocrat is better and better." Mrs. Stowe's story, "The Minister's Wooing," first appeared in this paper and helped to reach a larger circle of readers.

From a financial point of view the *Atlantic* was of great assistance, paying Whittier better than any of his other work had done. In Mr. Fields, the publisher, Whittier had a good friend who, knowing the poet's heart was much bigger than his pocket, and that when he wanted to do liberal things he had to refrain, sent him the following charming little note:

Let me whisper to you, if at any time you find your pocket light, it will give me great pleasure personally to shovel in a few " rocks," to be returned at any time when most convenient to you, or if they should never come back it would be better still. My hand is still lame, but I can sign a cheque at any time if a friend needs it.

The first numbers of the *Atlantic Monthly* contained some of Whittier's best known poems, such as "The Gift of Tritemius," "Skipper Ireson's Ride," "The Old Burying Ground," "Telling the Bees," "The Swan Song of Parson Avery," as well as legends and ballads, all to become historic.

In the autumn of 1857 Whittier lost his mother. He was stunned by the bereavement, and he wrote to Sumner :

I have been watching by the bedside of my dear mother, following her in love and sympathy to the very entrance of the valley of shadows. She is no longer with us. The end was one of exceeding peace, a quiet and beautiful dismissal. The world looks far less than it did when she was with us. Half the motive power of life is lost.

There was a beautiful bond of union between mother and son, but though the wrench was great Whittier did not indulge in idle sorrow.

The nations at that time were watching with intense interest the struggle for liberty which was going on in Italy. Of course Whittier was keen in his admiration for Garibaldi, and he wrote a fine eulogium on the hero; and other poems flowed from his pen in which he expresses the intensity of feeling against all tyranny.

"From Perugia," "The Prisoners of Naples," "The Dream of Pio Nono," "Italy," and others, express his love to towards all those who suffered in the cause.

Remembering others, as I have to-day,
In their great sorrows, let me live alway
 Not for myself alone, but have a part,
Such as a frail and erring spirit may,
 In love which is of Thee, and which indeed
  Thou art.*

In the year 1860, a Republican Mass Meeting was held in Newburyport. There was a sense of anxiety as to the vote for Pennsylvania. Whittier felt a crisis was coming, that an irrevocable choice was going to be made. "God grant that it may be rightfully made" he wrote. "Let us not be betrayed into threats. Leave violence where it belongs, with the wrong doers." He expressed in his poem "What of the Day?" his underlying fear that victory

* "The Prisoners of Naples."

was not to be gained by the ballot only, but that a more deadly struggle was at hand, and many a verse went forth laden with this burden on his mind.

> A sound of tumult troubles all the air,
> Like the low thunders of a sultry sky,
> Far-rolling ere the downright lightnings glare;
> The hills blaze red with warnings, foes draw near,
> Treading the dark with challenge and reply.

If the Quakers could be roused, Pennsylvania could be counted on to return Abraham Lincoln. Whittier was stirred and wrote "The Quakers are out!" to be sung at the meeting, the leaflet being headed, "A Voice from John G. Whittier."

THE QUAKERS ARE OUT!

> Not vainly we waited and counted the hours,
> The buds of our hope have all burst into flowers.
> No room for misgiving—no loop-hole of doubt—
> We've heard from the Keystone! The Quakers are out.
>
> The plot has exploded—we've found out the trick;
> The bribe goes a-begging; the poison won't stick.

When the Wide-awake lanterns are shining about
The rogues stay at home, and the true men are out !

The good State has broken the cords for her spun ;
Her oil-springs and water won't fuse into one ;
The Dutchman has seasoned with Freedom his krout.
And slow, late, but certain, the Quakers are out !

Give the flags to the winds ! set the hills all aflame !
Make way for the man with the Patriarch's name !
Away with misgiving—away with all doubt,
For Lincoln goes in, when the Quakers are out !

In November, 1860, Lincoln was elected. Whittier was devoutly thankful, though anxious. The air was filled with suggestions how best to propitiate the people in the Slave States whose "inordinate demands" it seemed impossible to meet. Whittier strongly upheld a plan, suggested by Sumner, of compensation on the part of the government for the emancipation of slaves in any State that was prepared to abolish the curse of slavery, for he felt it would show that their hatred was not towards the slave holders but towards slavery.

To W. S. Thayer he wrote, "The South by their madness are assuming all the responsibility of whatever painful duty may be imposed upon the government. It may be the will of God that slavery shall perish through their folly and crime. If so, all the people will say, Amen."

Certain of the clergy and politicians were trying to compromise in order to save the Union. To Whittier, who had said "*Backbone* is the greatest thing needed," this was little short of treason. He was roused to unusual ire by Parson Adams' words in a book then issued, and said to Lydia Maria Child :

It is the foulest blasphemy that was ever put in type, but weak as it is wicked. Get it ; it is a curiosity of devilish theology worth studying. What is to be the end of this disunion turmoil ? I cannot but hope that, in spite of the efforts of politicians and compromises, the Great Nuisance is to fall off from us ; and we are to be a free people.

CHAPTER IX

ON Abraham Lincoln assuming office, in March, 1861, it was known that slavery would not be tolerated any longer in the North and West. This started a rebellion in the Southern States, when it was resolved that they should break away from the Union, and eleven States seceded.

The people of the North rose to defend the Union, and the war spirit was let loose. Whittier prayed:

" Give us grace to keep
   Our faith and patience; wherefore should
     we leap
On one hand into fratricidal fight
Or, on the other, yield eternal right.

" We must be first pure, then peaceable." This is the Christian rule of life, and though Whittier tells us he was born without an atom of patience, he tried to manufacture it as needed, and as far as we can tell his success was very satisfactory. But it was a sore trial to his spirit to keep calm at this time, though he wrote :

> God reigns, and let the earth rejoice !
> I bow before His sterner plan.
> Dumb are the organs of my choice;
> He speaks in battle's stormy voice,
> His praise is in the wrath of man.*

The older members of the Society of Friends were in a "strait betwixt two," for, while they had to bear their testimony against all war, they had duties as citizens on behalf of their country; and many of their sons, whose sympathies were strongly against all slavery, had enlisted in military service to fight, as they believed, a righteous cause.

Whittier showed them the more excellent way in an address he penned " To Members of the Society of Friends."

In this circular, dated 18th 6th mo., 1861, he says,

We have no right to ask or expect an exemption from the chastisement which the Divine Providence is inflicting upon our nation. Steadily and faithfully maintaining our testimony against war, we owe it to the cause of truth to show that exalted heroism and

* "Italy."

generous self-sacrifice are not incompatible with our pacific principles. Our mission is at this time to mitigate the sufferings of our countrymen, to visit and aid the sick and the wounded, to relieve the necessities of the widow and the orphan, and to practise economy for the sake of charity. Let the Quaker bonnet be seen by the side of the black hood of the Catholic Sister of Charity in the hospital ward. Let the same heroic devotion to duty, which our brethren in Great Britain manifested in the Irish famine and pestilence, be reproduced on this side of the water in mitigating the horrors of war and its attendant calamities. What hinders us from holding up the hands of Dorothea Dix* in her holy work of mercy at Washington? Our Society is rich, and of those to whom much is given much will be required in this hour of proving and trial.

How his heart must have been bowed down as neighbours and friends with whom he had held sweet converse met on the battle-field, some on one side, some on the other, to shoot each other down, for with Whittier war was nothing short of murder.

Notwithstanding, he wrote verses that stirred the soldiers, and a message was sent him from one of the regiments saying,

* An American philanthropist.

"Your verses have made us all your friends, lightening the wearisomeness of our march and brightening our lonely camp fires."

The slaughter on the battle-field, the "glory," so called, of the struggle, was only sad and *in*glorious to Whittier, but he tried to keep before the men the greatness of the cause, the sin of slavery and the desire to put an end to injustice and oppression.

In *The Atlantic*, there appeared a poem by Whittier which created a great sensation, and over which there has been a good deal of controversy. Some, with the present-day love of questioning everything, have denied the fact on which the story is founded; but since Whittier has left on record that the poem was written "in strict conformity to the account of the incident" as he had it from respectable and trustworthy sources, and as convincing proofs came to him of the accuracy of the narrative, we can leave the matter there.

When Lee's army occupied Fredericktown the only Union flag displayed was held from an upper window by Barbara Frietchie, a widow aged 97 years.

Every store was closed, and the dwelling-houses also. The streets were lavishly decorated, but the most conspicuous object was the grey head of the old lady holding her flag from her attic window, and waving it as the troops passed by.

> Up rose old Barbara Frietchie then,
> Bowed with her fourscore years and ten;
>
> Bravest of all in Frederick town,
> She took up the flag the men hauled down;
>
> In her attic window the staff she set,
> To show that one heart was loyal yet.
>
> Up the street came the rebel tread,
> Stonewall Jackson riding ahead.
>
> Under his slouched hat left and right
> He glanced; the old flag met his sight.
>
> " Halt ! "—the dust-brown ranks stood fast,
> " Fire ! " out blazed the rifle-blast.
>
> It shivered the window, pane and sash;
> It rent the banner with seam and gash.
>
> Quick, as it fell from the broken staff
> Dame Barbara snatched the silken scarf.
>
> She leaned far out on the window-sill,
> And shook it forth with a royal will.
>
> " Shoot, if you must, this old grey head,
> But spare your country's flag," she said.

A shade of sadness, a blush of shame,
Over the face of the leader came;

The noble nature within him stirred
To life at that woman's deed and word.

" Who touches a hair of yon grey head
Dies like a dog! March on!" he said.

The heroic old lady died a few days after from the excitement of the event and the lionization which followed it. When the poem was sent to Mr. Fields for insertion in *The Atlantic*, Whittier received the following characteristic reply: "A proof will be sent you in a few days. You were right in thinking I should like it, for so I do, as I like few things in this world. Inclosed is a cheque for fifty dollars, but Barbara's weight should be in gold."

In the spring of 1862, Whittier received the welcome news of the abolition of slavery in the District of Columbia—the first fruits of what was to follow. This had been considered by him as an imperative duty, and he writes to Sumner:

Glory to God! Nothing but this hearty old Methodist response will express my joy at the passage of the bill for the abolition of slavery in the District in the Senate of the United

States. I hail it as the first of the "peaceable fruits of righteousness" which are to follow the chastening of war, which now for the present "seemeth grievous." It is a great event, a mighty step in the right direction. I can now lift up my head without shame in the face of the world. I am thankful that Massachusetts was well represented in the Senate—that to her belongs so much of the honour of the noble achievement.

Whittier was sending forth poem after poem, leading the hearts of the people in "Thy Will be Done" to see how the highest can only be obtained through the cross, and that with joy even we must bear the burden, that God's designs may be wrought out. The closing verses ring out a holy confidence in His will :

> If, for the age to come, this hour
> Of trial hath vicarious power,
> And, blest by Thee, our present pain,
> Be Liberty's eternal gain,
>   Thy will be done!

> Strike, Thou the Master, we Thy keys,
> The anthem of the destinies!
> The minor of Thy loftier strain,
> Our hearts shall breathe the old refrain,
>   Thy will be done!

The poem "Ein' feste Burg ist unser Gott" followed, again turning the hearts of men to the strength of God, who through "the pains of purifying" can bring peace. "The Battle Autumn of 1862," "Astræa at the Capitol," and others, were redolent of the truth that the right *must* win. He "knew that truth would crush the lie," but, as he said, "The *Truth* can wait."

He, nevertheless, was only too conscious of the shortcomings of the people, and expresses himself thus:

God only knows whether we really deserve success in this terrible war. When I think of the rapacity of contractors and office holders, and of the brutal and ferocious prejudice against the poor blacks, I almost despair; so far as we, the whites of the North, are concerned, God's will be done whatever becomes of us.

Some Englishmen were criticising in no friendly manner the struggle going on against slavery. To Whittier this was a matter of intense indignation, and in hot haste he wrote:

You flung your taunt across the wave;
We bore it as became us,

Well knowing that the fettered slave
Left friendly lips no option save
  To pity or to blame us.

You scoffed our plea. 'Mere lack of will,
  Not lack of power,' you told us:
We showed our free-state records; still
You mocked, confounding good and ill,
  Slave-haters and slave holders.

O Englishmen! in hope and creed,
  In blood and tongue our brothers!
We too are heirs of Runnymede;
And Shakespeare's fame and Cromwell's deed
  Are not alone our mother's.

We bowed the heart, if not the knee,
  To England's Queen, God bless her!
We praised you when *your* slaves went free;
We seek to unchain ours. Will ye
  Join hands with the oppressor?

And is it Christian England cheers
  The bruiser, not the bruisëd?
And must she run, despite the tears
And prayers of eighteen hundred years,
  Amuck in slavery's crusade.[*]

But we see the man's fine nature in that, while his spirit was stirred with indignation at the injustice of the accusations brought

[*] "To Englishmen."

against his countrymen, he was ready in a moment to show his sympathy with the many in our own country who were suffering through the American War.

There was much distress owing to the scarcity of the cotton supply. If at the commencement of the struggle the cotton had been seized, as was suggested, and sent off to England before the blockade, it would have been much better for the South and for the manufacturing districts.

Whittier, on hearing of the distress and of collections being made for the relief of the sufferers, succeeded in raising $238 in Amesbury, and forwarded the amount to John Bright with grateful appreciation of his generous efforts to promote good feeling between the peoples of England and the United States.

John Bright's acknowledgment is worth preserving, in which he says :

27th, 2mo., 1863.—Thy letter has given me much pleasure. The contributions I have paid over to the relief fund. I am sure the kindness towards our people indicated by the contributions has given much pleasure in many quarters. . . I have been a warm admirer and a constant reader of thy poems for many years, and I can imagine something of the deep interest which the great conflict must excite in thee. It seems as if a peaceable termination of the great evil of slavery was impossible. The blindness, the pride, and the passion of men made it impossible. War was, and is, the only way out of the desperate difficulty of your country, and fearful as is the path, it cannot be escaped. I only hope there may be virtue enough in the North, notwithstanding the terrible working of the poison of slavery, to throw off the coil, and to permit of a renovated and restored nation. With us, we are witnessing a great change of opinion, or opinions hitherto silent are being expressed. In every town a great meeting is being held to discuss the " American question," and the vote is almost everywhere unanimously in favour of the North. The rich and the titled may hate the Republic, but the *people* do not. I await tidings from the States with anxiety, but I have faith in freedom and in good.

Better times financially were coming to the poet. His volume *In War Time* was selling well, and we find him acknowledging a remittance which he tells his publisher " makes me rich as Crœsus—I am like one who, counting over his hoards, finds it double what he expected."

During the national struggle, which was nearing its end, Whittier was to lose his life-long companion, his sister Elizabeth. She passed through some months of distressing illness borne with great patience and cheerfulness even to the last, but on 3rd September, 1864, Whittier wrote to her great friend, Lucy Larcom :

Our dear Lizzie is no longer with us. She passed away this morning. Notwithstanding her great weakness, I find I was not prepared for the event. It is terrible—the great motive of life seems lost. We were friends before thee knew my sister ; but now all who loved her, and whom she loved in turn, are nearer and dearer to me. I feel it difficult to realize all I have lost, but I sorrow without repining, and with a feeling of calm submission to the Will which I am sure is best.

The relationship of Whittier with Lucy Larcom was one of spiritual affinity. He had helped her to see the Invisible, to believe in a future life, to know that " death doth hide but not divide those who are on Christ's other side." In one letter he had received from her she said: " Every year it seems a happier thing to be alive and to know that I cannot die. Through *thee*, my friend, I have come to see this very slowly."

Thus to turn to Lucy seemed to be his great consolation. He had ever been thoughtful for her, and enriched her life in many ways, and now it was Miss Larcom's privilege to solace the bereaved brother as none other was able to do. She had Elizabeth's portrait painted and presented it to the poet, and it became one of his dearest treasures.

The first poem written after his sister's death was "The Vanishers," from a beautiful legend in Indian mythology of little people who received and lost their lives according to their usefulness, and Whittier thought of it in connection with his loss as he says:

> Gentle eyes we closed below,
>   Tender voices heard once more,
> Smile and call us, as they go
>   On and onward, still before.
>
> Chase we still, with baffled feet,
>   Smiling eye and waving hand,
> Sought and seeker soon shall meet,
>   Lost and found, in Sunset Land!

CHAPTER X

IN the early spring of 1865 the passing of the constitutional amendment, abolishing slavery, was at hand.

One morning, in the Quakers' Meeting House, where Friends gathered in the middle of the week for an hour of worship—the ringing of bells and the roar of cannon startled the quiet assembly, and Whittier knew that the work to which he had set his heart and hand during the best years of his life was accomplished. In the silence of the meeting he gave thanks, and as he sat there, the poem he called "Laus Deo" "sang itself," as he said, "while the bells rang."

> It is done!
> Clang of bell and roar of gun
> Send the tidings up and down.
> How the belfries rock and reel!
> How the great guns, peal on peal,
> Fling the joy from town to town.

> Let us kneel;
> God's own voice is in that peal,
> And this spot is holy ground.
> Lord, forgive us! What are we,
> That our eyes this glory see,
> That our ears have heard the sound!

But his beloved Lizzie was not with him to see and to hear, to rejoice and be glad!

They had worked together in this great cause. When he was inclined to be desponding she could always cheer him with her bright and brave words, and how he must have longed to share this joy with her. He had said "I miss dear Elizabeth to enjoy the beauty of the autumn woods with me." How much more to rejoice with him in the abolition of slavery, in the consummation of their dearest hopes; but he could say, not only with the lips but in sincerity, "That which He allots to us, or our friends, is for the best." Happy man to have learned that lesson by *heart*!

The Amesbury home was now very desolate after Whittier's great loss, but he said to Lucy Larcom: "If I can help it, I do not intend the old homestead to be gloomy and forbidding through my selfish regrets. She would not have it so. She would wish it cheerful with the old familiar faces of the friends whom she loved and still loves."

But naturally his mind turned to his old home not six miles away, to the happy family, the faces he had loved, the voices he longed to hear, to the long winter evenings of the past, when, snowed up, the story telling would enliven the quiet hours. As he thought upon these things consecrated by memory, he found profit and joy in lingering over the old days, and the idyl was called forth which he named "Snowbound," sketching with graphic pen the scenes of his youth and the beautiful love which united father, mother, children and friends in holiest bonds. Could nobler and more beautiful words express his faith in the future life than those he penned when thinking of his loved ones who had passed away, and of whom he dreamed as he wrote?

> Their written words we linger o'er,
>   But in the sun they cast no shade,
>   No voice is heard, no sign is made,
> No step is on the conscious floor!
> Yet Love will dream, and Faith will trust,
> (Since He who knows our need is just,)
> That somehow, somewhere, meet we must.

> Alas for him who never sees
> The stars shine through his cypress-trees!
> Who, hopeless, lays his dead away,
> Nor looks to see the breaking day
> Across the mournful marbles play!
> Who hath not learned, in hours of faith,
>   The truth to flesh and sense unknown,
> That Life is ever lord of Death,
>   And Love can never lose its own!

In October, 1865, the manuscript was sent to his friend and publisher, Mr. Fields, "to do with as seemeth best in thy sight." So "Snow-bound" was born into the world. It is Whittier's most familiar poem, and his description of his home, his family, and his friends has become the typical picture of winter life in that bright clime, but "nature is subordinated, even at nature's height of power, to human character."*

The book was a literary and financial success, expressing as is thought Whittier's highest genius. The author received through the profits of the first issue ten thousand dollars. While thankfully acknowledging this surprising remuneration, his heart could not but sorrow that it had not come earlier in life, when he would have

* "American Men of Letters," by Carpenter.

"SNOWBOUND": THE HOMESTEAD IN WINTER.

had the joy of ministering more generously to the mother and sister, who had passed from his sight without having enjoyed the comforts he had always longed to lavish upon them. In reference to this, he wrote to a friend, Margaret Burleigh :

I thank thee for thy kind note of congratulation upon my supposed riches. I *have* been favored more than I ever dreamed of, however. This enables me to meet the extra expenses of living, and to send my niece to Ipswich Seminary . . When it pleases the Lord to call me, I shall leave little to quarrel about among my relatives. If my health allowed me to write I could make money easily now, as my anti-slavery reputation does not injure me in the least, at the present time. For twenty years I was shut out from the favor of booksellers and magazine editors, but I was enabled by rigid economy to live in spite of them, and to see the end of the infernal institution which proscribed me. Thank God for it.

The " infernal institution " having come to an end left him more free for quiet thoughts and musings, and some of his best work was done after he had passed the three score years.

The next volume of poems issued bears the title of "The Tent on the Beach," a summer story stringing together several ballads, some unpublished and others which had appeared in *The Atlantic*.

"'The Tent on the Beach' is not pitched yet," he wrote to his publisher, "nay, more, the very cloth of it is not woven"; but four months later the manuscript was forwarded. "Put it in type or on the fire, I am content, like Eugene Aram, prepared for either fortune."

Fields, quite satisfied, went to press with it, and on sending the book to Whittier received for answer:

The Tent looks well. I like thy part of it. Mine, I see, needs some corrections and emendations. But if, as *The Transcript* says, you have been foolish enough to print ten thousand copies, there will never be a chance for that. It will never come to a second edition. I hope there is some mistake about it; I should not like to see your shelves loaded with unsold verses.

As it turned out, the twenty thousand copies of the book were quickly sold, some thousand a day being called for.

This was communicated to Whittier who exclaimed :

Think of bagging in this " Tent " of ours an unsuspecting public at the rate of a thousand a day ! This will never do. The swindle is awful. Barnum is a saint to us. I am bowed with a sense of guilt, ashamed to look an honest man in the face. But Nemesis is on our track ; somebody will puncture our "Tent" yet, and it will collapse like a torn balloon.

Notwithstanding, it went off joyfully, and was received by the " unsuspecting " public with enthusiasm.

In 1867 the public, ever on the scent for the sensational, circulated the report that Mr. Whittier was about to be married.

His friends at this time filled a large place in his life, many of them women with whom he kept up a vigorous correspondence. Still to Lucy Larcom, probably his closest friend because so dear to his sister Elizabeth, he cries out :

Credulity, thy name is woman. So thou believed that report almost! Well, the first intimation of it came to me through the newspapers. *They* ought to know. I can't imagine how or where it started. It vexed me, but of course there was no help for it.

And to another he says :

The idea of offering matrimonial congratulations to a hopeless old bachelor trying to thread a needle to sew on his buttons! As well talk of agility to a cripple, or of a rise in government stocks to a town pauper. Of course, thee didn't believe the silly story. I wish the newspaper scamp who started it nothing worse than to be an old bachelor like myself, or to have a wife like Mrs. Caudle.

The story may have arisen through a piece of advice administered by a worthy woman, who on calling upon Mr. Whittier was told two more were waiting for him in the parlour. "What, more of them," she exclaimed, " was ever man so beset ? But it's good enough for you. You should have married a woman long ago, and *she* would have kept all the rest off ! "

His correspondence was a continued tax on his time. Some fifty letters would arrive by the morning post; but much of the brightness of his life in later years came from his epistolary effusions with interesting people such as Oliver Wendell Holmes, Phillips Brooks, Lucy Larcom, Lydia Maria Child, Emerson, James Fields and his wife, Lowell, Mrs. Stowe, Elizabeth Stuart Phelps,

Edna Dean Proctor, Celia Thaxter, Mrs. Claflin and many another.

Possibly his delicate health, his dislike of tobacco, and wine, and sport, isolated him somewhat from robust manhood and made his friendships very largely among the gentler sex.

At that time the question of female suffrage was exciting considerable interest in the States, and Whittier was asked to attend a Convention at Newport. His reply on the whole subject is interesting and well balanced, and deserves careful thought:

Amesbury (Mass.),
12th, Eighth Month, 1869.

My dear Friend,—I have received thy letter inviting me to attend the Convention on behalf of Woman's Suffrage at Newport, R.I., on the 25th inst. I do not see how it is possible for me to accept the invitation, and, were I to do so, the state of my health would prevent me from taking such a part in the meeting as would relieve me from the responsibility of seeming to sanction anything in its action which might conflict with my own views of duty or policy. Yet I should do myself great injustice if I did not embrace this occasion to express my general sympathy with the movement. I have seen no good reason why mothers, wives and daughters should not have the same right of person, property, and citizenship which fathers, husbands and brothers have.

The sacred memory of mother and sister; the wisdom and dignity of women of my own religious communion, who have been accustomed to something like equality in rights as well as duties; my experience as a co-worker with noble and self-sacrificing women, as graceful and helpful in their household duties as firm and courageous in their public advocacy of unpopular truth; the steady friendships which have inspired and strengthened me; and the reverence and respect which I feel for human nature, irrespective of sex, compel me to look with something more than acquiescence on the efforts you are making.

I frankly confess that I am not able to foresee all the consequences of the great social and political change proposed, but of this I am at least sure—it is always safe to do right, and the truest expediency is simple justice. I can understand, without sharing, the misgivings of those who fear that, when the vote drops from woman's hand into the ballot-box, the beauty and sentiment, the bloom and sweetness of womanhood will go with it. But in this matter it seems to me we can trust Nature. Stronger than statutes or conventions, she will be conservative of all that the true man loves and honours in woman. Here and there may be found an equivocal, unsexed Chevalier d'Eon, but the eternal order and fitness of things will remain. I have no fear that man will be less manly or woman less womanly when they meet on terms of equality before the law.

On the other hand, I do not see that the exercise of the ballot by women will prove a remedy for all the evils of which she justly complains. It is her right, as truly as mine, and when she asks for it, it is something less than manhood to withhold it. But, unsupported by a more practical education, higher aims, and a deeper sense of responsibilities of life and duty, it is not likely to prove a blessing in her hands any more than in man's.

With great respect and hearty sympathy,
I am very truly thy friend
JOHN G. WHITTIER.

Whittier's kindly nature, his sympathy with humanity everywhere, endeared him to those in the humble walks of life, as well as those in his own circle, and he was continually planning for the happiness of those about him.

His washerwoman, who by thrift and industry had been able to build herself a little house, must have a house warming, thought Mr. Whittier; so he planned it all and the neighbours arrived with their presents, and he made a little speech and said he would "read a piece of machine poetry which had been intrusted to him for the occasion":

>Of rights and of wrongs
>Let the feminine tongues
> Talk on—none forbid it.
>Our hostess best knew
>What her hands found to do,
> Asked no questions, but DID IT.
>
>Here the lesson of work,
>Which so many folks shirk,
> Is so plain all may learn it;
>Each brick in this dwelling,
>Each timber is telling
> If you want a home, EARN IT.
>
>Thanks, then, to Kate Choate!
>Let the idle take note
> What their fingers were made for;
>She, cheerful and jolly,
>Worked on late and early,
> And bought—what she paid for.
>
>Never vainly repining,
>Nor begging, nor whining;
> The morning-star twinkles
>On no heart that's lighter,
>As she makes the world whiter
> And smooths out its wrinkles.

On another occasion there was what he called a "surprise party" at the house of an old man in humble circumstances, who had received a nice little sum of money from many of his neighbours, and in the village paper there was a notice of it as follows : "A vote of thanks was passed to Mr. Whittier as the originator of the party, but that gentleman begged leave to disclaim all merit in the matter :—it was not his or anybody's doing,—it grew out of its own fitness,—it made itself and came there of its own accord."

Whittier knew the secret source of happiness and revealed it to others, as when in a letter to Celia Thaxter he said, "I am glad to learn that thee are making thyself happy in making others so. Probably there is no other way. My happiness has pretty much come in that manner and my unhappiness from the selfish pursuit of enjoyment to the neglect of duty."

But one likes to think that he had "lots of nice books and pictures" and many friends he could make merry with—though sometimes questionable friends pursued him and he could have cried out with Shakespeare, "Weak we are and cannot shun pursuit," for autograph collectors would call by day and by night, and though always desiring to be kind, he had sometimes to leave them in the lurch.

One evening, after he had retired to bed, a party of students arrived, each with an autograph book in hand. They apologized for being late through having lost their train, but would Mr Whittier write his name in their books? Whittier rose and dressed himself, and descended the stairs, to find his house fairly filled with young men, and he at once sat down to do their bidding. On leaving with profuse thanks, one of the number looked into his book and exclaimed, " Oh, you have only written John in my book!" "I am afraid some of you have not got as much as that," said Whittier, as he took up his candle and bade them " good-night."

Not able to leave home on account of his health, many friends gathered round him and kept him in touch with the outer world. Together they discussed the literature of the day, for Whittier was a voluminous reader.

To Edna Dean Proctor he talked of oriental poetry and religion, a subject of intense interest to him ; of the Mohammedans, and their silent spiritual worship, of the Greek Church and Clement of Alexandria.

Elizabeth Stuart Phelps called forth a favourite theme—the future life and its requirements. He said to her one evening, when they were together in semi-darkness as the twilight fell, discussing the destiny of the impenitent, "Elizabeth, thee would never be happy in heaven unless thee could go as missionary to the other place now and then."

His keen interest in the welfare of the slave was a strong bond of union between himself and Harriet Beecher Stowe, and she and the poet would sometimes sit till the small hours of the morning talking of the political horizon, the prospects of emancipation, psychical mysteries and ghost stories upon which the lady would dilate with personal intuition. With a professed touch of jealousy, Whittier would mourn that the spirits would follow her bidding but always left him severely alone.

Then there were other visitors who gave an encouraging word on parting, as did Charles Kingsley, who said, "Mr. Whittier, I want to tell you how much we all love you ; everything you write is read in England ; my wife is never without a volume of your poems by her side."

Whittier spoke of patience as a rare commodity in his nature, but the " manufacturing business " of cultivating it was certainly a successful one, though now and again he was caught in a fit of impatience. But what antagonist could resist the following apology after a breezy encounter with a friend, and do aught but laugh over it afterwards ? :

Thee are right in thinking that I don't know much about what was said on the evening thee refers to. If I remember rightly thee was unreasonably persistent in thy contention. When one is unreasonable himself he is in no mood for tolerating the same thing in others. I dare say that I was a fool, but that is no reason thee should make thyself one by dwelling on it. Lay it all to dyspepsia, Ben Butler, or anything else than intentional wrong on the part of thy old friend. We have known each other too long, and done each other too many kind offices, to let it disturb us.

In 1871 Whittier edited *The Journal of John Woolman*, of whom Charles Lamb wrote " Get the writings of John Woolman by heart ; and love the early Quakers."

This was a task which we can easily understand was very agreeable to the poet. He was eminently fitted to portray the character of one so selfless yet so human, fearlessly fighting the love of gain and the injustice of slavery. One who in his youth had the courage to say to his master that slave-keeping was inconsistent with the Christian religion. How like in a measure to Whittier's own life, for John Woolman never, though strongly condemning the iniquity of slavery, lost sight of the oneness of humanity. Whittier closes his introduction in these beautiful words :

In bringing to a close this paper, the preparation of which has been to me a labour of love, I am not unmindful of the wide difference between the appreciation of a pure and true life and the living of it, and am willing to own that in delineating a character of such moral and spiritual symmetry I have felt something like rebuke from my own words. I have been awed and solemnized by the presence of a serene and beautiful spirit, redeemed of the Lord from all selfishness, and I have been made thankful for the ability to recognise, and the disposition to love him.

CHAPTER XI

IN 1876 Whittier's niece, who had lived with him since his sister's death, was married, leaving him once again a lonely old man. His three cousins, and their father Colonel Edmund Johnson, were anxious that he should remove to Oak Knoll and make their house his home.

"Oak Knoll" was a farm of sixty acres, between Boston and Newburyport, with twenty acres of lawn and numerous fine trees. It was supposed to be haunted since one of its former occupants had suffered death as a wizard two hundred years before.

Whittier's cousins were very warmly attached to him and no arrangement could have been more suitable and pleasant than the one suggested.

Whittier agreed to live with them for the greater part of the year, retaining his cottage at Amesbury for the sake of its associations, and that he might return to it now and again on a long visit. Soon after he had taken up his abode at the Knoll the Colonel died, and Whittier naturally came in many ways to occupy his place, and received the tender care the daughters had been in the habit of bestowing on their beloved father.

"Oak Knoll," the name given to the estate by Whittier, was to a lover of nature a sweet home, with its picturesque hills, its grassy knoll, its orchards, its cedars, and moss covered rocks. He would wander along the groves and return laden with wild flowers.

Every season of the year brought some special charm to him. He enjoyed the quiet with the songs of the birds, and sang his own songs as his thoughts rose to the Creator of all beauty, and the God of all love.

> And I will trust that He who heeds
>   The life that hides in mead and wold,
> Who hangs yon alder's crimson beads
>   And stains those mosses green and gold,
> Will still, as He hath done, incline
> His gracious care to me and mine;
> Grant what we ask aright; from wrong debar,
> And, as the earth grows dark, make brighter
>   every star!*

* The Last Walk in Autumn.

The season that to many is regarded as a sad one, when autumn ushers in the deep sleep of winter, was to Whittier one of special glory with its tinted leaves, its galaxy of colour: scarlet maples, russet beeches, yellow hickories, golden walnuts and graceful silvery birches.

> Touched by a light that hath no name,
>   A glory never sung,
> Aloft on sky and mountain wall
>   Are God's great pictures hung.
> How changed the summits vast and old!
>   No longer granite-browed,
> They melt in rosy mist; the rock
>   Is softer than the cloud.*

If the dawn was clear, he always rose to witness the rising of the sun. That marvel and mystery of creation, the rising and the setting sun, brought him very consciously into touch with the love and beauty of God, and he worshipped as he gazed thereon.

In speaking of "Oak Knoll," he said, "I am satisfied with this." A sense of thankfulness rests with us as we remember that the long years of struggle and poverty were crowned in the eventide of life with the utmost comfort and peace.

*"Sunset on the Bearcamp."

Here he wrote descriptions of country life, of sunset and ocean, of storm and calm, hymns and visions of beauty, tributes of respect to those whom he had honoured, and also one of the most beautiful of his poems, " Revelation."

Here, he received frequent visitors from far and near, Dr. Goldsmith, Oliver W. Holmes, Paul Hayne the poet, Sir Edwin Arnold, Bishop Brooks, Dorothy Dix the beloved philanthropist, and many another.

Dorothy Dix spent a summer in the neighbourhood of Amesbury, and she and Whittier were frequently together. They had much in common, both had worked in putting wrongs right and in ministering to others. Whittier, in his old age, to the spiritual needs of mankind, Dorothy to the material needs of life.

Whittier's hymns were greatly treasured by her, and when she was dying his poem " At Last " was never far from her side. It was in her hand by day, and under her pillow by night, and was laid in her hand at last and buried with her.

The year after Whittier had settled down at " Oak Knoll," his seventieth birthday came round and was the occasion of great rejoicing. The publishers of *The Atlantic Monthly* gave a dinner in Boston to which they invited leading poets and authors. Emerson, Longfellow, O. W. Holmes, Howells, Clemens (Mark Twain), with many literary friends not so well known on this side of the water made up a party of over sixty guests.

O. W. Holmes recited a poem in which he had described Longfellow, Emerson, Lowell and Whittier with touches of humour and sympathetic notes of appreciation. He closed with the following lines on Whittier :

> And the wood-thrush of Essex—you know whom I mean,
> Whose song echoes round us while he sits unseen,
> Whose heart-throbs of verse through our memories thrill
> Like a breath from the wood, like a breeze from the hill,
> So fervid, so simple, so loving, so pure,
> We hear but one strain, and our verdict is sure,—
> Thee cannot elude us,—no further we search,—
> 'Tis holy George Herbert cut loose from the church !
> We think it a voice of a seraph that sings,—
> Alas, we remember that angels have wings :—

What story is this of the day of his birth?
Let him live to a hundred! we want him on
  earth!
One life has been paid him (in gold) by the
  sun;
One account has been squared and another
  begun;
But he never will die if he lingers below
Till we've paid him in love the balance we
  owe.

Mark Twain was intensely comic and irresistible. Mrs. H. B. Stowe wrote of Whittier being a true poet whose "*life* is a poem." The president of Harvard College said "They who love God will thank Him from their hearts for the tenderness and simple trust with which Whittier has sung of the Infinite Goodness."

As time went on, the friendship with Dr. Oliver Wendell Holmes increased, and his visits to "Oak Knoll" were greatly prized and enjoyed by both. "They sat by the fireside, or walked through the lawns with arms entwined behind each other's backs,—rare old boys" whose hearts were young again.

Whittier was the elder by two years, and enjoyed the fun of proclaiming his priority. "Why, thou art a boy yet, while I am now four score."

"Ah," said the Doctor, "I called upon a lady yesterday who is several years older than either of us. Confound it, Mr. Whittier, these women will get the better of us some way. That's the reason why they hung them in old times. It was the only way the men could get even with them."

The friendship with Oliver Wendell Holmes was one of the "supreme luxuries of life." There was a freemasonry, a mutual understanding between them, when flashes of wit or raillery, "measure for measure," mingling with laughter, was often followed by earnest converse on the hereafter.

The letters from O. W. Holmes which have been preserved are delightful. On receipt of one of Whittier's volumes of poems he writes:

Boston, Oct. 10, 1878.

My dear Whittier,—I know how to thank you for the poems, but I do not know how to thank you for the more than kind words which make the little volume precious. I never was so busy, it seems to me, what with daily lectures and literary tasks on hand, and all the interruptions which you know about so well. But I would not thank you for your sweet and most cheering remembrance before reading every poem over, whether I remembered it well or not. And this has been a great pleasure to me, for you write from your heart and reach all hearts. My wife wanted me to read one,—a special favourite of my own,—" The Witch of Wenham," but I told her " No." I knew I should break down before I got through with it, for it made me tearful again, as it did the first time.

I was going to say I thank you, but I would say rather, I thank God that He has given you the thoughts and feelings which sing themselves as naturally as the wood-thrush rings his silver bell,—to steal your own exquisitely descriptive line. Who has preached the gospel of love to such a mighty congregation as you have preached it? Who has done so much to sweeten the soul of Calvinistic New England? You have your reward here in the affection with which all our people, who are capable of loving anybody, regard you. I trust you will find a still higher, in that world the harmonies of which find an echo in so many of your songs.

Then again on 6th March, 1881, he writes:

I have sweetened this Sunday afternoon by reading the poems in the precious little volume you sent me a few days ago. Some were new to me, others, as you ought to know, are well known. I have not forgotten your kind words for my evening breakfast. If you happen to have seen an article in the March — or was it February? — *North American,* you will have noticed, it may be, my reference to "The Minister's Daughter," and to yourself as preaching the Gospel of Love to a larger congregation than any minister addresses. I never rise from any of your poems without feeling the refreshment of their free and sweet atmosphere. I may find more perfume in one than in another — as one does in passing from one flowery field into the next. I may find more careful planting in this or in that, as in different garden-beds, but there is always the morning air of a soul that breathes freely, and always the fragrance of a loving spirit. Again that sweetest "Minister's Daughter" brought the tears into my eyes — and out of them. Again I read with emotion that generous tribute ["The Lost Occasion"] to the man whom living we so longed to admire without a reservation — of whom dead you write with such a noble humanity. I must not speak too warmly of the lines whose kindness I feel so deeply, only wishing I had deserved such a tribute better. But of the poem which comes next, "Garrison," I can speak, and I will say that it has the strenuous tone, the grave music of your highest mood, — which I believe is the truest and best expression of the New England inner life which it has ever found, at least in versified utterance. I have forgotten to thank you for remembering me, and especially for the way in which you remember me, for I did not miss the words which made my blood warm, as I read them on the fly-leaf. Let me say—for it means more than you can know—that no written or printed words come into our household on which my wife, a very true-hearted woman, looks with so much interest as on yours.

One more, written on 18th October, 1881, must suffice :

I have worn the same glasses for twenty years. I am getting somewhat hard of hearing—" slightly deaf " the newspapers inform me, with that polite attention to a personal infirmity which is characteristic of the newspaper press. The dismantling of the human organism is a gentle process more obvious to those who look on than to those who are the subjects of it. It brings some solaces with it ; deafness is a shield ; infirmity makes those around us helpful ; incapacity unloads our shoulders ; and imbecility, if it must come, is always preceded by the administration of one of nature's opiates. It is a good deal that we older writers, whose names are often mentioned together, should have passed the Psalmist's limit of active life, and yet have an audience when we speak or sing. I wish you all the blessings you have asked for me—how much better you deserve them!

When Sir Edwin Arnold visited him, they talked long on the themes of life and immortality. Canon Farrar, Bishop Brooks, and many New England friends, spent happy hours at the Knoll. Delegates from the Society of Friends in Great Britain came and held spiritual converse with the poet, when "after greetings and congratulations were delightfully dispensed, a silence would fall upon the small company and every voice would be hushed. One, or another, moved by the Divine Spirit, would at times speak words of counsel, comfort, or admonition, to those present, often closing reverently with prayer."

Life was growing very easy to Whittier, as the shadows lengthened. He was able to enjoy the comforts which surrounded him, and the kind care bestowed upon him by his cousins. His only burden was that his correspondence increased as he was less able to bear it, for his kindly nature urged him to do more than he had strength for.

The applications for verses and autographs were constant; and poor authors, and youthful literary aspirants, sought advice as to how they might become famous. Whittier was always gentle in his dealings with them, and if he saw any sign of talent he gave encouragement, but he never advised any to start verse making for a livelihood.

In 1885 Whittier was asked by Mr. Reed to write an ode to the memory of General Gordon. This request presented considerable difficulty, owing to ill health on the one hand and his peace principles as a Friend on the other, but he had followed Gordon's course with intense interest and he spoke of him as a "Providential man; his mission in an unbelieving and selfish age revealing the mighty power of faith in God, self-abnegation and the enthusiasm of humanity."

He declined the offer, wishing it were in his power to do what had been requested, and suggesting that Alfred Tennyson be approached to give the world a "threnody inspired by the life and death of one who had not only made England, but the world, richer for his memory."

Tennyson responded, though not writing as much as Whittier hoped.

Dear Mr. Whittier.—Your request has been forwarded to me, and I herein send you an epitaph for Gordon in our Westminster Abbey— that is, for his cenotaph :—

> "Warrior of God, man's friend, not here below,
> But somewhere dead far in the waste Soudan,
> Thou livest in all hearts, for all men know
> This earth hath born no simpler, nobler man."

With best wishes, yours very faithfully,*
TENNYSON.

In an English paper it was said that Whittier offered no objection to writing an ode on a soldier, and this brought a long letter in protest to the poet from John Bright.

This incident would not be referred to but for the answer sent to Bright by Whittier, which is interesting on account of the views expressed on several points, and also for the broad-minded way in which he judged matters, so far removed from the sectarian spirit which at times influences the best of men.

* Pickard, 707.

(To John Bright) 31. 3 mo, 1885.

My dear Friend,—I regret the publication of my hasty note to C. Reed, as it has occasioned thee uneasiness. I quite agree with thee as regards the armed interference with Egypt and the Soudan, and I think one of the best acts of thy life was thy withdrawal from the ministry in consequence of it. But as respects Charles Gordon, I cannot withdraw my admiration from the man, while I disapprove of his warlike methods. I learned much of him from my friend Dr. Williams, who knew him well in China, and who thought him one of the most generous and self-sacrificing men he ever knew. Still later, I have read of his labors in the Soudan to suppress the dreadful slave trade, and it seems to me that he went to Khartoum once more really on an errand of peace, and I am not sure that he would not have succeeded if the English army had not invaded the Soudan. It is not probable that I shall write a poem on his life and death, but I thought of it, and intended to express my admiration of his faith, courage and self-abnegation, while lamenting his war training and his reliance on warlike means to accomplish a righteous end. As it is, he was a better man than David or Joshua—he was humane, and never put his prisoners into brick-kilns nor under hammers. And he believed in a *living*

God, who reveals himself now, as in old time. There seems to be no excuse now for keeping General Wolseley in the Soudan. I see no reason for fighting the Arabs, who surely are not to blame for disliking the rule of Egypt. I hope the danger of a war between England and Russia has passed away. The matter at issue is one to be settled by arbitration, not by the sword. I wish we could say that my country is Christian. Our new Secretary of State has spoken out manfully and strongly against the dynamite mischief. The past winter has been a hard one for me, and I am far from well. Hoping that thy own health is good, I am, with love and sincere regard, thy friend,

J. G. WHITTIER.

Whittier was quite firm on the peace question. It was always a subject of intense sorrow to him that the struggle for Freedom had been attained through such terrible slaughter, and he questioned if the end justified the means. "If I could have foreseen," he said, "the dreadful bloodshed which resulted from the great conflict, I should have hesitated and restrained my ardor for a more peaceful solution of the great problem."

The knowledge that the poet had not lived to make his name known, or laboured legitimately to cultivate an art for the enjoyment and applause of his countrymen, but that he had buried his pardonable ambition, and devoted his life to serve and liberate his fellowmen from bondage, brought him the respect, the reverence and the affection of multitudes.

Thus a most interesting interview took place with Dom Pedro, the Emperor of Brazil, who had for many years followed Whittier's poems with deep interest and translated several into Portuguese. On his visit to the United States, when Whittier was living at Oak Knoll, he expressed his great desire to see Longfellow and Whittier. Whittier in his turn was equally desirous to meet the Emperor, knowing him to be a distinguished philanthropist, but the difficulty was how it could be arranged. Whittier wrote to Mr. Fields, " If he could only do as other folks do, I should like to have thee and Mrs. Fields escort him here, where we could see him apart from the fuss and feathers of ceremony for an hour or two. But owing to the 'divinity that doth hedge a king,' that can't be of course. He is a splendid man, let alone his rank and title."

They got over the difficulty in this way. He was invited to a private parlour to meet some of the famous Boston men of letters, and Mrs. Claflin, who was present, gives an account of the interview.

As one after another was presented to him the Emperor received each graciously, but without enthusiasm. But when Mr. Whittier's name was announced, his face suddenly lighted up, and grasping the poet's hand, he made a gesture as though he would embrace him, but seeing that to be contrary to the custom of the country, he passed his arm through that of Mr. Whittier and drew him gently to a corner, where he remained with him, absorbed in conversation until the time came to leave. The Emperor, taking the poet's hand in both his own again, bade him a reluctant farewell and turned to leave the room, but still unsatisfied, he was heard to say, "Come with me," and they passed slowly down the staircase, his arm around Mr. Whittier.

CHAPTER XII

AFTER his eightieth birthday had passed, Whittier received a request to write a quatrain for a memorial window to the honour of John Milton to be placed in St. Margaret's Church, London, the Church of the House of Commons in which he had worshipped.

George W. Childs, of Philadelphia, a great admirer of Milton's works, entrusted Archdeacon Farrar with a sum of money for that purpose. It was a munificent gift, and the window is exceedingly beautiful both in design and colour.

When it was nearly finished, the Archdeacon wrote to Mr. Childs, saying he could think of no one so suitable as J. G. Whittier to write four lines for the memorial, Lowell having responded to a like request for the Raleigh window.

Whittier was pleased and sent the following lines :

The new world honors him whose lofty plea
  For England's freedom made her own more sure,
Whose song, immortal as its theme, shall be
  Their common freehold, while both worlds endure.

Dr. Farrar sent a delightful acknowledgment :—

Jan. 2, 1888.

First let me express the wish that God's best blessings may rest on you and your house during this New Year. My personal gratitude and admiration have long been due to you for the noble influence you have exercised for the furtherance of forgotten but deeply needed truths. I have myself endeavoured to do something to persuade men of the lesson you have so finely taught—that God is a loving Father, not a terrific Moloch. Next let me thank you for the four lines on Milton. They are all that I can desire, and they will add to the interest which all Englishmen and Americans will feel in the beautiful Milton window. I think that if Milton had now been living, you are the poet whom he would have chosen to speak of him, as being the poet with whose whole tone of mind he would have been most in sympathy.

Bishop Brooks and Farrar had spent a very enjoyable day with Whittier when the Archdeacon was visiting the United States, and the memory of it was treasured by both the great men. Phillips Brooks speaks of how much he had to thank the poet for, " very much indeed," as he says.

But old age was becoming more and more exacting in its demands upon the already enfeebled condition of the poet, whom we find writing of " nervous debility," and his difficulty in " holding his thoughts together," and in the evenings he was not able to read as had been his wont. Still, life was a joy to him, and in the spring-time on a fresh morning he would call to his cousins, " Come, put on your wraps and all go with me for a walk."

His letters, too, never ceased to be of keen interest to him. The services he had rendered, the inspiring words he had written, brought acknowledgments of gratitude, and offerings of affection, often from most unexpected quarters as well as from fast friends.

One, a bachelor, touched to tears in reading " Snowbound," expressed his indebtedness in the following words :

New York.

Mr. John G. Whittier,

My dear Sir,

I am a stranger to you personally, but have long been familiar with your intelligence and spirit, your poetry being a darling of my heart, which I have hugged closely for years. My admiration must at least be deemed impartial, for I am a Catholic and know what you have written about Pio Nono. I was a Democrat of the Southern class, and know how much your thoughts did to keep alive the effort, which I thank God has resulted in the abolition of slavery. I am of Irish parentage, and it is a source of great pleasure and mirth to my friends and myself that I can challenge all the literature of Erin to furnish one description so thoroughly Irish as your portrait of Hugh Tallant in the "Sycamores." I think it is the most racy and rollicking as well as truthful representation of the Milesian that ever came to my notice. You have learned long since that Tom Moore did not write poetry, but treats Irish subjects with oriental imagery. The poets of '48, particularly Tom Davis, have done much better, but the odor of the brogue is stronger in Hugh Tallant than in even their pictures.

I am impelled to address you because I have just wiped from my eyes the tears called to them by your "Snow-bound," and from the bottom of my heart I thank you for the spiritual enjoyment you have furnished in this exquisite poem, and for your grand idea—

"That life is ever Lord of Death,
And Love can never lose its own."

I hope you will be pleased to know that a lawyer of fifty years old, and an old bachelor at that, still keeps alive in his soul the most undying fondness for poetry. As to being an old bachelor, I care little for that now, seeing how gracefully you have presented an old maid in your last sweet production.
Yours very truly,
JAMES T. BRADY.

A cheery note came from Oliver W. Holmes, who was so near Whittier's age and who had just passed his eightieth birthday:

Here I am at your side among the octogenarians. At seventy we are objects of veneration; at eighty of curiosity, at ninety of wonder; and if we reach a hundred we are candidates for a side show attached to Barnum's great exhibition. You know all about it. You know why I have not thanked you before this for your beautiful and precious tribute, which would make any birthday memorable. I remember how you were overwhelmed with tributes on the occasion of your own eightieth birthday, and you can understand the impossibility I find before me of responding in any fitting shape to all the tokens of friendship which I receive. I hope, dear Whittier, that you find much to enjoy in the midst of all the lesser trials which old age must bring with it. You have kind friends all around you, and the love and homage of your fellow-countrymen as few have enjoyed, with the deep satisfaction of knowing that you have earned them, not merely by the gifts of your genius, but by a noble life which has ripened without a flaw into a grand and serene old age. I never see my name coupled with yours, as it often is nowadays, without feeling honoured by finding myself in such company and wishing that I were more worthy of it.

His birthdays were now the landmarks in the life of Whittier, for as his writings were becoming more widely known, each 17th of December brought an increasing knowledge of the many he was guiding to a nobler life. This was deep joy to him, and the "blessed mood" lingered and sealed the peace he had always endeavoured to maintain.

When he was eighty-two years of age he received as a birthday present a beautiful glass vessel, containing gold sand from Africa, the golden cover being ornamented with a clasp of diamonds and a fine sapphire, in memory of his self-sacrificing work for freedom.

Letters and gifts arrived also from all parts of the States, and he was deeply touched by the remembrances from the students of the coloured seminary.

His next birthday brought him over three hundred letters, one of them coming from his friend Helen Keller, the deaf and blind girl, whose wonderful ability and genius is now so well known. She wrote in the square characters she had been taught to make:

Dear kind Poet,—This is your birthday; that was the first thought which came into my mind when I awoke this morning, and it made me glad to think I could write you a letter and tell you how much your little blind friends love their sweet poet and his birthday. . . If I were with you to-day I would give you eighty-three kisses, one for each year you have lived. Eighty-three years seems very long to me. Does it seem long to you ? I am afraid I cannot think about so much time. I hope your Christmas day will be a very happy one, and that the new year will be full of brightness and joy for you and everyone.

From your loving little friend,

HELEN A. KELLER.

Whittier was still able to enjoy writing, and the following year he published for private circulation a little volume of poems written in his old age, which he called " At Sundown."

The inevitable separations, which lengthened life brings to all who have passed the fourscore years, were teaching Whittier that he too must soon enter the unknown land, and when James Russell Lowell died, in 1891, the poet speaks of the event in a letter to Oliver W. Holmes:

The bright beautiful ones who began life with us have all passed into the great shadow of silence, or in the language of Vaughan, " They have gone into the world of light, and we alone are lingering here, but the world is still fair to me ; my friends are very dear. I love and am loved."

He knew he was nearing the end of the earthly pilgrimage, for he had been ill through the summer, and his own beautiful words, expressed in " The Eternal Goodness," must often have been with him as he thought of putting out to sea, of the "muffled oar," the unknown "islands," the weakness of the flesh overcome by the confidence of faith that

> No harm from Him can come to me
> On ocean or on shore.

So he could wait, for he knew with a most holy assurance that he could never drift from the Father's loving care.

The last birthday came round with its usual love tokens of fruit and flowers, eighty-four roses being tied with a scarf on which pictures of his early home had been painted.

Numbers of friends arrived, and Phillips Brooks sent the following message:

> I have no right save that which love and gratitude and reverence may give to say how devoutly I thank God that you have lived, that you are living, and that you will always live.

A telegram arrived from an Indian poetess of Ontario, another from several hundred students in Vassar College, and the pupils of a High School sent an affectionate greeting "to our loved singer, the wood-thrush of Essex."

Dr. Holmes never forgot his friend, and his welcome remembrance could always be reckoned upon on these anniversaries :

I congratulate you upon having climbed another glacier and crossed another crevasse in your ascent of the white summit which already begins to see the morning twilight of the coming century. A life so well filled as yours has been, cannot be too long for your fellow men. In their affections you are secure, whether you are with them here or near them in some higher life than theirs. . . We are lonely, very lonely in these last years. The image which I have used before this in writing to you recurs once more to my thought. We were on deck together as we began the voyage of life two generations ago. A whole generation passed, and the succeeding one found us in the cabin, with a goodly number of co-evals. Then the craft which held us began going to pieces, until a few of us were left on the raft pieced together of its fragments. And now the raft has at last parted, and you and I are left clinging to the solitary spar which is all that still remains afloat of the sunken vessel. Of many who are dead you are the most venerated, revered, and beloved survivor ; of these few living, the most honoured representative. Long may it be before you leave a world where your influence has been so beneficent, where your example has been such inspiration, where you are so truly loved, and where your presence is a perpetual benediction.

The day passed happily, and Whittier seemed hardly fatigued when the last guest departed; and he dwelt at the evening meal on the delight of meeting with his friends and the happy day he had spent.

As the summer arrived he proposed spending a few weeks with Sarah Gove at Hampton Falls, about seven miles from Amesbury, and he went off in good spirits, saying as he started : " I shall not be gone over three weeks, and when I get back we will have the Whittier Club here from Haverhill. I want them to see me here, among the trees where I have had so much pleasure and comfort."

He went by way of Amesbury, where he remained a few days and then on to Hampton. The house, its surroundings, and his friends made it a rare treat to visit Hampton. It was associated with memories of his mother. The landscape was magnificent and he spent many happy hours on the wide balcony opening out from the door of his room.

"This is a very sweet spot to me," he said one day, when in the midst of a group of young people; and when his cousin asked if he intended going on to Centre Harbor, as he had purposed doing, he replied, "I have been thinking about it, but have given it up, it is so pleasant here, and we are having such a comfortable, happy summer."

August was passing, and towards its close he had one of the usual attacks which at that time of year he had been liable to. On recovering he spoke of returning to Newburyport, but on September 3rd he had a slight stroke and was obliged to return to bed.

He had always expressed a desire to die in the old home at Amesbury, but when he realized that the end was not far off and he could not be moved, he expressed himself as perfectly content. "It is all right and everybody is so kind."

One incident, so characteristic of the man, should not be passed by, even though it mars the peace and beauty of the surroundings of that death-bed.

A letter came from a stranger addressed to Whittier, upbraiding him for his rudeness in not acknowledging a volume which had been sent him. The letter was read to the poet, and he replied : " The poor man does not know the circumstances, which must be explained to him *pleasantly*, and directions must be sent to my publishers to have a volume of my works forwarded to him."

The correspondent received the notice of Whittier's death with the letter and book, following a telegram announcing that his letter had been sent to a dying man.

Whittier's strength was rapidly failing. When his medicine was taken to him he said, "It is of no use ; I am worn out "; then he repeated " Love, Love to all the world," and that was the thought resting with him to the end.

His blinds were always drawn up that the first ray of light might come to him. He who loved the Light of Heaven, loved also the light of day. And in the early morning of 7th September, 1892, as the first rosy hues of colour were stretching across the horizon, he who seemed quietly sleeping passed into the eternal Light.

One of the little group of his loved ones, as they surrounded the bed, recited his own beautiful poem, " At Last " :

When on my day of life the night is falling,
  And, in the winds from unsunned spaces blown,
I hear far voices out of darkness calling
  My feet to paths unknown.

Thou who hast made my home of life so pleasant,
  Leave not its tenant when its walls decay ;
O Love Divine, O Helper ever present,
  Be Thou my strength and stay !

Be near me when all else is from me drifting ;
  Earth, sky, home's pictures, days of shade and shine,
And kindly faces to my own uplifting
  The love which answers mine.

I have but Thee, my Father ! let Thy spirit
  Be with me then to comfort and uphold ;
No gate of pearl, or branch of palm I merit,
  Nor street of shining gold.

Suffice it if—my good and ill unreckoned,
  And both forgiven through Thy abounding grace—
I find myself by hands familiar beckoned
  Unto my fitting place.

Some humble door among Thy many mansions,
  Some sheltering shade where sin and striving cease,

And flows forever through heaven's green
    expansions
  The river of Thy peace.

There, from the music round about me
    stealing,
I fain would learn the new and holy song,
And find at last, beneath Thy trees of healing,
  The life for which I long.

When his death was known, the flags on the public buildings were raised half-mast and the bells rang out eighty-four strokes.

The Mayor of Haverhill issued a proclamation in which he said, after stating the fact of J. G. Whittier's death :

As a man of letters the world bears record of his fame. His purity of thought and life, his compassion for the unfortunate, and his heart that was ever open for his kind, stamp him as one who will receive the honor and homage of every nation and every tongue. But to us, the people of the city that gave him birth, there is a still tenderer tie. Our hills, our woods, our lakes, and our traditions furnished themes for his gifted pen. Nay, we have felt the strength of his citizenship and the warmth of his love, and it is with peculiar and heartfelt sorrow that we mourn for our own.

On the 8th of September, Whittier was removed to the old home at Amesbury, where he was placed in the memorable sitting-room beneath the portraits of his mother and sister. He had expressed in his will his desire to be buried in the simple and plain manner of the Friends, and this was carried out.

The gathering at the funeral was held in the garden, the house being far too small to receive the hundreds of people who assembled to express their regard and affection for their poet and friend.

The Whittier family had been laid to rest side by side in the Friends' portion of the burial ground. Father, Mother, two sisters, Aunt Mercy, and Uncle Moses. Plain stones, exactly alike, mark their resting places. Of Whittier's stone his old friend Oliver Wendell Holmes wrote :

> Lift from its quarried ledge a flawless stone ;
>   Smooth the green turf and bid the tablet rise,
> And on its snow-white surface carve alone
>   These words—he needs no more—*here Whittier lies.*

And of the spirit of the poet he adds :

Death reaches not a spirit such as thine,—
　It can but steal the robe that hid thy wings;
Though thy warm breathing presence we resign,
　Still in our hearts its loving semblance clings.

CHAPTER XIII

THERE is no need to enlarge much on the foregoing sketch of J. G. Whittier's life, but some words should be added as to his personality, his character, and his future position as a poet.

The portraits of Whittier are unfortunate. He disliked the process and said, " If there is anything I shrink from with especial terror it is to be made a picture or graven image of," and the " terror " seems to have crept into nearly all the likenesses. The one selected for the frontispiece is the most pleasing the writer could find.

Whittier was tall, very erect, slightly built, " with the reticence and presence of an Arab chief."* His complexion was slightly olive, his eyes deep set with strongly marked eyebrows, the eyes remarkable for their intensity, and a poet's mouth, lips nervous but resolute.

* T. W. Higginson.

Mrs. Pitman, daughter of Judge Minot, describes him at the age of nineteen as a "very handsome distinguished looking young man." He was careful in his dress. His coat in later life was a perfect fit, and his outer one, with fur collar, was very becoming, "which fact some of his women friends suspected he knew as well as they."

His chief characteristics are spoken of as due mainly to his Quaker birth and training. He was very modest, quite conscious of his limitations even after he had made a name in the world.

Naturally ambitious, his Christianity enabled him to lay it aside that he might serve mankind in an unpopular cause. He aspired after congressional honours when a young man, and had a fair prospect of attaining his desire, and it is thought that his sacrifice has not been sufficiently estimated.

His poetry was influenced by the sacrifice he made, and gained much, as we have seen, through the purity of his motives and life.

He never flattered anyone, and would at times give wholesome advice in a manner which did not give offence, a gracious art peculiar to the typical saintly members of the Society of Friends.

He was strong in character and courageous enough to act according to his conscience, regardless of consequences which might earn any measure of unpopularity.

He was quiet in company, but with his intimate friends very genial and amusing, with the ready wit characteristic of the Whittier family, and no party in the neighbourhood was thought complete without the poet, owing to his popularity. Those who were privileged to spend an evening with him, never forgot his charming vivacity and confidences, his retentive memory and large fund of information on many subjects making him very good company. The editor of *The Bookman* tells of a visit to Whittier a few years before his death, and the description of the poet is very graphic :

His face had none of the immobility so frequent with very aged persons; on the contrary, waves of mood were always sparkling across his features and leaving nothing stationary there except the narrow, high and strangely receding forehead. His language, very fluid and easy, had an agreeable touch of the soil, an occasional rustic note in its elegant colloquialism that seemed very pleasant and appropriate, as if it linked him naturally with the long line of sturdy ancestors of whom he was the final blossoming. In connection with his poetry, I think it would be difficult to form in the imagination a figure more appropriate to Whittier's writings than Whittier proved to be in the flesh.*

He was a safe counsellor, and could work with anyone without quarrelling if they were trying to forward a good cause even though not in his way, and he cultivated the widest charity for every honest opponent.

Towards individuals he was tender, but towards wickedness he was stern as the Hebrew prophets of old in his deep and almost terrible indignation.

He lived through stirring times when men's passions were roused, and we realize what an effort it was for him to keep calm even with his unusual power of self-control.

" I wonder," he said, " whether the old saints when invested with robes and sanctity found it so difficult as I do to walk in them. Jordan is a hard road to travel. Only a day or two ago

* *The Bookman*, viii., p. 459.

I lost my temper because someone who was not a saint, but only an average church member, was perverse and ill dispositioned; and I disputed the bill of an Irishman who thought it right to make sport of a Protestant Egyptian, and I dare say he went away with no satisfactory evidence of my saint's life."

In his poem " My Namesake " he speaks of himself thus :

> Few guessed beneath his aspect grave
> What passions strove in chains.

In reviewing Whittier's position as a poet, any criticism accentuating " cultured fastidiousness " finds no place in the purpose of this biography.

The variety of opinion is somewhat wide. Perhaps G. R. Carpenter expresses most justly his power when he says : " In form his poetic product is characterized by extreme simplicity and his skill is due to native talent. Of American poets he appeals with Longfellow to the plain people, to the major part of the inhabitants of the land. Both were, in spite of great differences in education and experience, singularly simple-minded men. . . Both were by nature singers, and for the nation at large none of their contemporaries can compare with either."

He closes by saying : " He was so strictly a local poet that it is doubtful of what permanent value he will be to other nations using our common language, but with us his fame is secure."

Whittier, unlike most poets, seems to have done his best work in his later years. His Quaker training restrained him in the early period from that romantic passion and sensuous joy which often excites true genius. Later on he was so absorbed in the Anti-Slavery cause that his creative energy is chiefly controlled by the stern call of a reformer with a prophet's " burden."

Someone has said, " He was born a soldier and made over into a Quaker, and the soldier knocks the Quaker down now and then." Certainly his war poems stirred the blood. The following is a good example :

>   What gives the wheat-field blades of steel ?
>   What points the rebel cannon ?
>   What sets the roaring rabble's heel
>   On the old star-spangled pennon ?
>   What breaks the oath
>   Of the men o' the South ?

What whets the knife
For the Union's life ?
Hark to the answer : Slavery !

In his later years the depth of his spiritual nature and vision is seen in exquisite simplicity and beauty, as in " The Eternal Goodness," " Our Master," " Revelation," " At Last," and many another.

We venture to think that Whittier is growing in the hearts of the English speaking people everywhere. His poems have crept into many collections without the author's name appearing. His hymns are sung by worshippers of varied creeds.

In " Worship Song," a collection of hymns for public worship by W. Garrett Horder, there are more of Whittier's than those of any other poet.

As in the works of John Ruskin, his words will live not because of the art he cultivated but for the great principles of truth and love which he has expounded.

Ruskin has given us underlying principles as the foundation of his art; Whittier has given us underlying principles as the foundation of his religion; and it is becoming more and more evident that the

Christian religion is built up upon principles that are the outcome of the spirit of Christ, in which a whole world can unite, and not upon a creed or letter of Scripture.

John Bright wrote of Whittier : " It is a great gift to mankind when a poet is raised up amongst us who devotes his great powers to the sublime purpose of spreading amongst men principles of mercy, justice, and freedom. This our friend Whittier has done in a degree unsurpassed by any other poet who has spoken to the world in our noble tongue."

It is not alone that the greatest genius lives ; but the man who lives in the hearts of the people leaves thoughts that fructify, that produce other thoughts that are lived out in other lives, and continue to bless mankind.

Criticism will change, " our little systems have their day," but by such a thought as the following Whittier must live :

> By all that He requires of me,
> I know what God Himself must be.

Only a few simple words, but containing a world of meaning.

W. Garrett Horder, the hymnologist, expresses what is likely to be the final verdict concerning Whittier's position in this country. "Probably," he says, "his most poetic, and therefore most enduring work is to be found in Poems, Subjective and Reminiscent; and in his Religious Poems, where his keenly ethical, and at the same time deeply spiritual, nature finds fullest expression. In these there is a simplicity, a reality, a pathos of expression all too rare in verse of this order."*

An incident, a thought, came to Whittier, and he would embody it in a few verses that carried it into the spiritual world and taught a lesson such as could not be easily forgotten.

The following is an illustration and a gem of its kind :

THE LIGHT THAT IS FELT.

A tender child of summers three,
 Seeking her little bed at night,
Paused on the dark stair timidly,
 "Oh, mother! take my hand," said she.
  'And then the dark will all be light."

---

* Preface to Oxford edition of "J. G. Whittier's Poems."

We older children grope our way
  From dark behind to dark before ;
And only when our hands we lay,
Dear Lord, in Thine, the night is day,
  And there is darkness nevermore.

Reach downward to the sunless days
  Wherein our guides are blind as we,
And faith is small, and hope delays ;
Take Thou the hands of prayer we raise,
  And let us feel the light of Thee !

In his poem " Among the Hills " we have one of his most beautiful idyls in its simple description of scenery and rustic country life.

Whittier was a mystic, and a seer. The invisible world was the influence in his life ; the spiritual world the reality. Life was one beautiful whole, no hard and fast division of secular and sacred troubled him. The fruit of the spirit could grow out of every action : every meal was a sacrament, every place was holy, every human being could be the temple of the Holy Ghost.

He was full of pity for men and women bowed down with the sins and sorrows of life, ever lifting their burdens, and helping to share them; and those who gathered about him found a sense of peace and joy. That was the atmosphere of his home, and made the true spirit of worship a reality, expressed in his own words:

O brother man! fold to thy heart thy brother;
  Where pity dwells, the peace of God is there;
To worship rightly is to love each other,
  Each smile a hymn, each kindly deed a prayer.

The prophetic gift was his also. He was a seer. Not in the sense of foretelling coming events, but in speaking God's will, and testifying to the certain future of those things that are noble and right, and of those that are base and cruel. We can never foresee how any of our actions are going to work out in particulars, but we do know that God's laws never fail, and the warnings of the old prophets on breaking those laws made men feel the terror of evil doing. Whittier never spared the wicked act, or held back its inevitable consequence on the wrong-doer. The ripe fruit of iniquity he left no doubt would be bitterness indeed, as the ripe fruit of all righteousness, peace and joy.

> Breathe forth once more those tones sublime
>   Which thrilled the burdened prophet's lyre,
> And in a dark and evil time
> Smote down on Israel's fast of crime
>   The gift of blood, a rain of fire ! *

It is this beautiful and Christ-like combination of strength and gentleness, manliness and meekness, hatred of wrong and passionate love of righteousness, that made his life and teaching a strength and inspiration.
Oliver Wendell Holmes said Whittier's influence through his poems on the religious life of America had been greater than that of any preacher ; and his poems represent his life, for he wrote as men are prompted to pray. And as the strength and sweetness of his life has gone forth to purify the lives of many both here and in America, this appreciation has been written in the hope, and with the prayer, that others may be helped onwards and upwards in the Divine life, to live more nobly :

> Knowing this, that never yet
> Share of Truth was vainly set
>   In the world's wide fallow;

* "The Sentence of John L. Brown."

After hands shall sow the seed,
After hands from hill and mead,
  Reap the harvests yellow.

Thus, with somewhat of the Seer,
Must the moral pioneer
  From the Future borrow;
Clothe the waste with dreams of grain,
And, on midnight's sky of rain,
  Paint the golden morrow!*

---

* " Barclay of Ury."

CHAPTER XIV.

IN the year 1838, Great Britain passed the great Emancipation Act which then abolished slavery in all her Colonies and possessions.

The following is an extract from the Act :

That from the 1st day of August, 1838, all and every the persons hitherto held in Slavery within any British Colony shall be to all intents and purposes free and discharged of and from all manner of slavery and shall be absolutely and for ever manumitted,—and that the children to be born of such persons and the offspring of such children shall in like manner be free from their birth, and that from and after the 1st of August Slavery shall be and is hereby utterly and for ever abolished throughout the British Colonies, Plantations and Possessions.

In the year 1890 the Anglo-German Agreement was signed which ceded to Germany the Island of Heligoland, situated in the North Sea, in exchange for the Islands of Zanzibar and Pemba and a coast strip of the adjacent mainland of Africa (the dominions of the Sultan of Zanzibar).

It was not at first realized by our countrymen that, owing to the existence of slavery in the Sultanate, England had again, though inadvertently, become tainted with the evils of slavery.

The fact, however, was soon discovered by the friends of freedom in Great Britain, and in the year 1897 the Society of Friends appointed a Committee to deal with this iniquity. Meetings were held, and an agitation was promoted, demanding emancipation.

An industrial mission was started on the Island of Pemba in order to obtain accurate information as to the condition of the slaves, and also that work might be given them on their liberation.

The Foreign Office was pressed frequently to aid in the emancipation, and after twelve years of strenuous effort freedom was proclaimed, and we were again happily clear of the curse of slavery in our own possessions.

But we are not clear of this evil in cases where we have Treaty Rights with other nations. We are in some cases offering our protection where slavery is an institution. The honour of our country is at stake, and Archdeacon Potter goes so far as to declare that in this twentieth century things are transpiring which would not have been tolerated in the early Victorian era.

Appalling revelations have been made by such men as Mr. Nevinson, Mr. Swan, and Mr. Burtt (sent out by Messrs. Cadbury), of the cruelty and slavery in the Portuguese islands of San Thomé and Principe.

We have as a Nation Treaty obligations, 250 years old, covering these islands, and an undertaking from Portugal as late as 1890 for the total abolition of slavery in Africa.

Through numerous appeals to the Portuguese Government the transhipment of slaves from Angola has been arrested; but there are ominous signs that what has been done is to quiet the vigilance of the "Anti-slavery and Aborigines Protection Society," and that the old methods may come into force again. *The Spectator* has valiantly taken up this question and writes firmly and emphatically as follows :

Either the Portuguese must put an end to slave-owning, slave-trading, and slave-raiding, in the colonial possessions which we now guarantee to them, or else our guarantee must at once, and for ever, cease. It is utterly intolerable that we as a nation having always held, and rightly held, that the noblest thing in our history is the abolition of the slave trade throughout the world, and of slavery in our own dominions, should now be actually guaranteeing a condition of slavery in Portuguese Africa.

It is calculated that the slave population of 40,000 dies off within ten years, men and women it must be remembered in the prime of manhood and womanhood. When children are born they are taken from their mothers and become the property of the masters, and one overseer on the mainland of Angola stated that he had over one hundred young ones in the compound, just as a farmer would speak of his cattle.

The condition of things is intolerable, and the Anti-Slavery and Aborigines Protection Society, which exists for the very purpose of dealing with such a subject, is exerting its influence, with the aid and sympathy of many leading men, to see that justice is done to the natives. Mr. and Mrs. Harris have recently returned from a long and dangerous journey through the Congo, also visiting the Islands of San Thomé and Principe, and they tell us of a conversation between some of the natives and Mr. Harris. He asked them questions concerning their condition and their future prospects, and their replies were as follows :

" Yes, our food is all right ; we get clothes ; but we are badly flogged." I said to the young men, " But you look fairly healthy, and you know we are told in Europe that you are never beaten." " What, white man ? Never beaten," he responded, quite angrily, and added, " Tell me, what is this ? " And then he showed me a wound in the back of his head. " That," he said, " is the sort of thing we get from the ganger." Another bore the unmistakable evidences of sleeping sickness, and his life could not be prolonged a very great while. I asked these young fellows if they wanted to go home, and they replied, " White man, why do you ask us such a question ? We have no hope of going home. Did you ever know a black man that did not want to go home ? Why do you tantalise us by asking if we desire to go home ? " I said, " I will tell you why ; there are people in

Europe who care for your welfare and who, if you desire your freedom, will do their utmost to secure it for you." I added, " I am here to tell you that we will do our best to get you free " ; and then the spokesman turned on me and said, " White man, very soon you will be away beyond the great water there, and when you get on it you will forget all about the slaves on this island. We have nothing to live for." I replied, " Listen, and then pass the word round to the other slaves on the islands. I am going to Europe, and, God helping me, and helping the friends that are there, we will endeavour to set you free within two years."

" If you could realise," adds Mr. Harris, " that within five years 25,000 will have perished and within ten years 40,000 of them will have disappeared, I ask, whether it was a rash promise to make in the name of my Society that we will endeavour to set them free."

The humid climate of the islands is especially suitable for growing cocoa, and herein lies the danger, for the profits are great. Between the years 1897 and 1906 the cocoa production has trebled in quantity and doubled in value. The Portuguese authorities plainly tell us they have no intention of acting according "to the morbid mentality of exotic philanthropists."

But we, as a Christian nation, must ever bear in mind that a black skin should not forfeit any human being's right of freedom. God is no respecter of persons, He is equally Father of the black and of the white. He has endowed every one with certain inalienable rights, and where we are in any degree responsible it is our duty to see that justice is maintained.

If our Christianity is not strong enough to overcome this evil, which is contrary to the law of God, then it is not of God.

In Westminster Abbey we have buried one of our greatest heroes, David Livingstone, great, not so much as a scientist, or an explorer, but in his campaign against the slave system.

When Lord Palmerston in the name of his country sent to ask Livingstone what, as a nation, we could do for him to prove our admiration and gratitude for his services, his answer was as noble as the record of his life.

He asked nothing for himself, but sent an urgent request that arrangements might be made to secure the welfare of the slaves.

Livingstone's body was carried by his faithful followers and friends at the risk of their lives "over land and sea," that the great Doctor might "go home," these natives proving themselves by their fidelity, and self-sacrifice, worthy of our highest regard.

It is for such Livingstone asked our help; it is from such that freedom is withheld. The misery of slavery wrung his heart. He fought it single-handed. He wrote to his daughter, "From what I have seen of slavery I say exaggeration is a simple impossibility. I go with the sailor who on seeing slave traders said, 'If the devil don't catch them fellows we might as well have no devil at all.'" "The sights I have seen, common incidents of the traffic, are so nauseous, that I always try to drive them from my memory, but they make me start up at dead of night horrified by their vividness;" and in some of his last words, alone with God, he wrote, "May heaven's rich blessing come down on every one who will help to heal the open sore of the world." So much was he in sympathy with Whittier's struggle for Freedom that Stanley tells us, when spending those eventful months together in Darkest Africa, Livingstone would strengthen himself by repeating Whittier's poems, couplets of which were frequently heard. "Oh, when," he exclaimed, "shall the time come in which every man that feels the heat of the sun shall be free from all other fetters but the bonds of love?"

When?

When the spirit of J. G. Whittier and of Dr. Livingstone, that is the spirit of Jesus Christ, is found not here and there but in Christians everywhere. Then this accursed thing will cease from off the face of the earth.

> O speed the moment on
> When Wrong shall cease, and Liberty and Love
> And Truth and Right throughout the earth be known
> As in their home above.*

---

* " Clerical Oppressors."

INDEX.

Adams, Dr., 131.
Adams, John Quincy, 100.
Amesbury, 19, 75, 79, 80, 88, 162, 189, 194.
"Answer, The," 109.
Arnold, Sir, Edwin, 165, 172.
"Astræa at the Capitol," 64, 139.
"At Last," 165, 191-193, 202.
Atlantic Monthly, The, 125-127, 135, 137, 166.

Boston, Pro-slavery riots, in, 71, 72.
Brazil, Emperor of, 177, 178.
Bright, John, 141, 174-176, 203.
Brooks, Phillips (Bishop), 152, 165, 172, 181, 187.
Burns, Influence of, 30-32, 62.

Channing, Dr., 68.
Child, Lydia Maria, 131, 152.
Childs, George W., 179.
Coffin, Joshua, 30, 110, 111.
Collier, W. and W., 42-44.
Claflin, Mrs., 153, 178.

Cotton famine, 141.
Crandall, Dr. Reuben, 64.

Dix, Dorothea, 134, 165.

Emerson, 125, 126, 152, 166.
"Englishmen, To," 139.
"Eternal Goodness, The," 116, 186, 202.

Farrar, Archdeacon, 110, 172, 179-181.
Fields, James, 126, 137, 148, 150, 152, 177.
Friends, The Society of, 11, 14, 15, 102, 117, 129, 133, 145, 172, 194.
Frietchie, Barbara, 135-137.
Future Life, Poems and Thoughts on the, 92, 108-112, 143, 144, 147, 187, 192.

Garibaldi, 128.
Garrison, William Lloyd, 33-37, 42, 45, 59, 65, 71, 73, 82, 86.
Gordon, Suggested Ode to, 173-176.

Gove, Sarah, 189.
Grimké, Angelina, 83, 86.

Holmes, Oliver Wendell, 126, 165, 166-172, 183, 186, 188, 194.
Hooper, Lucy, 92-94.

"In Schooldays," 29.

Johnson, Col. Edmund, 162, 163.

Keller, Helen, 185.
Kingsley, Charles, 115, 159.

Larcom, Lucy, 78, 143, 144. 146, 151, 152.
"Laus Deo," 145.
Law, Jonathan, 50.
Light that is Felt, The, 204.
Lincoln, Abraham, 129, 130, 132.
Livermore, Harriet, 20, 24.
Longfellow, 125, 166, 200.
Lowell, James Russell, 96, 125, 152, 166, 186.
Lundy, Benjamin, 81, 82.

May, Samuel, 67, 71-73.
"Memories," 76.
Milton, Quatrain for memorial window to, 179, 180.

Oak Knoll, 162f.
"Our Master," 118, 202.

Page, Sophronia, 52.
Pedro, Dom, 177, 178.

Pennsylvania Hall burned, 82f.
Phelps, Elizabeth Stuart, 152, 159.
Philadelphia, 66, 82.
Procter, Edna D., 153, 158.

"Quakers are Out, The," 129.
Quakerism, *see* Friends, Society of.

"Revelation," 165, 202.
Russ, Cornelia, 56-58.

"Schooldays, In," 29.
Sewell, Samuel, 66.
Sigourney, Mrs., 54, 55.
Slavery Agitation, Anti-, 45, 59-100, 121-142, 145.
Slavery Declaration, Anti-, 67.
Slavery, Modern, 209-217.
"Snowbound," 16, 21-25, 79, 147-148, 181.
"Song of the Vermonters, The," 49.
Stowe, Mrs. Beecher, 99, 125, 126, 152, 159, 167.
Sturge, Joseph, 89-91, 112.
Sumner, Charles, 65, 97, 100, 107, 121-125, 130, 137.

Tennyson, Alfred, 173, 174.
Tent on the Beach, The, 150.
Texas Plot, The, 96.
Thaxter, Celia, 153, 157.

Index

Thayer, A. W., 37, 39, 42-44.
Thompson, George, 70, 71, 72, 74, 86.
"Thy Will be done," 138.

Weld, see Grimké.
Wendell, Ann, 94, 95.
Whittier, Abigail (*mother*), 18, 21, 32, 75, 127.
Whittier, Elizabeth (*sister*), 18, 22, 23, 71-73, 77, 143, 146.
Whittier, John (*father*), 18-21, 36, 37, 45, 46.
Whittier, John Greenleaf:
  Ancestry, 13-19.
  Birth, 18.
  Boyhood, 26-41.
  Anti-Slavery Work (*see under* Slavery).
  Farm sold and house bought at Amesbury, 75.
  Anti-Slavery poems published, 86.
  Poems, Political and "In War Time," 96, 129, 132, 133, 136, 138, 139, 142, 201.

Whittier, John Greenleaf:
  Poems on Italian Freedom, 127, 128.
  Outbreak of War, 132.
  Abolition of Slavery, 145.
  Removed to Oak Knoll, 162.
  Birthdays, 184-189.
  Visit to Hampton Falls, 189.
  Death, 190-195.
  Appearance, 40, 196-198.
  Character, 11, 38-40, 47, 48, 51, 55, 61, 65, 78-80, 91, 117, 140, 155, 160, 197-201, 205-207.
  Estimate of his work, 112, 200-207.
  Friendships, 94, 151-153, 158-160, 165, 167-172, 186-188.
  Peace principles, 133, 134, 173-176.
  Religious position, 101-113, 117-119, 138, 139, 202, 205.
Whittier, Mary (*sister*), 18, 22, 28, 32, 33, 35.
Women's Suffrage, 153.
"Woolman, Journal of John," 160, 161.